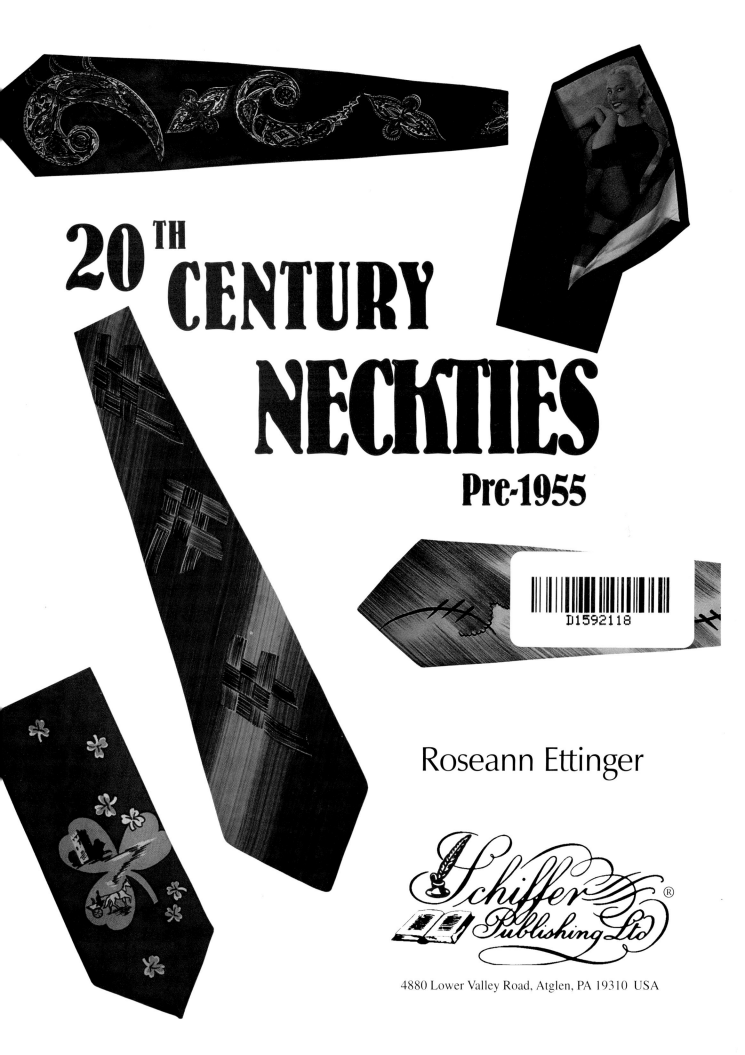

20TH CENTURY NECKTIES
Pre-1955

Roseann Ettinger

Schiffer Publishing Ltd

4880 Lower Valley Road, Atglen, PA 19310 USA

Dedication

To my Mother, Marie, for being the beautiful face on the necktie, and to my Father, Vito, for giving the tie to me when I was a little girl.

Designed by Laurie A. Smucker
Typeset in Zapf Humanist BT/Bernhard Bd Cn BT

ISBN: 0-7643-0578-6
Printed in China
1 2 3 4

Published by Schiffer Publishing Ltd.
4880 Lower Valley Road
Atglen, PA 19310
Phone: (610) 593-1777; Fax: (610) 593-2002
E-mail: Schifferbk@aol.com
Please write for a free catalog.
This book may be purchased from the publisher.
Please include $3.95 for shipping.

In Europe, Schiffer books are distributed by
Bushwood Books
6 Marksbury Avenue
Kew Gardens
Surrey TW9 4JF England
Phone: 44 (0) 181 392-8585; Fax: 44 (0) 181 392-9876
E-mail: Bushwd@aol.com
Please try your bookstore first.

We are interested in hearing from authors with book ideas on related subjects.

Contents

Acknowledgments 4

Preface 5

Introduction 6

Chapter I - The First 20 Years 20

Chapter II - The 1920s & 1930s 28

Chapter III - The War Years 1940-1945 46

Chapter IV - On The Wild Side 1945-1955 55

Bibliography 159

Acknowledgments

My sincere thanks to the following people who so graciously loaned me their favorite ties to be photographed for this book: Ann Rutten, Helen Nelson, Mark Zdancewicz, Laura Russell, Joe Polterak, Norvin McHose, Daphyn Shur, Regina Saunders, Dave and Meg Schneider, and Renee O'Connell.

Preface

Men's neckties have fascinated me since I was a child. My father's tie with my mother's picture hand painted on it was my inspiration. While my parents were on their honeymoon in 1950, the tie was painted by a street artist in New York City. I have treasured it for as long as I can remember.

As an adult, I began collecting men's ties in the early 1980s. Being in the vintage clothing business, however, I sold some very fine examples over the years before I realized that one day I would write a book about them. Unfortunately, some great hand painted examples slipped through my fingers before I ever had a chance to photograph them. The 1940s and 1950s abstract, geometric, and hand painted ties were always my favorites, but being somewhat of a historian, I decided to search for some earlier examples as well. About three years ago, I even found myself buying polyester kipper ties from the late 1960s and early 1970s, and designer and signature ties from the late 1970s and 1980s.

Collecting men's ties can be extremely entertaining and quite a bit of a treasure hunt, especially when you find that vintage example that might be signed "Dali"! If you are a man who thoroughly enjoys wearing ties, what a great way to express your personality. Whether it be a contemporary example, or one worn decades ago, a tie is wearable art.

Introduction

The origin of men's neckwear is a long and complicated history with many unanswered questions. A useless piece of fabric tied around one's neck has been a controversial topic for many years. Or was it useless?

Roman soldiers in the 2nd Century A.D. are depicted in a large marble sculpture in Rome called the Column of Trajan wearing linen scarves around their necks tied in various ways. Some of the scarves are tucked under the armour while others are tied similar to the modern four-in-hand necktie. This sculpture from antiquity depicts over 2,000 legionnaires wearing scarves around their necks. Was it part of their military uniform or used for protection against the elements? The answer is dubious.

In 1974, the tomb of China's first emperor, Shih Huang Ti, was uncovered near the city of Xi'an, the ancient capital of China. In the large tomb the famous "terracotta army" of 7,500 soldiers was also uncovered, each sculpted soldier was wearing a neckcloth. This piece of history dates back to 221 B.C. For centuries, the Romans were credited with the origin of men's neckwear until the 1974 discovery of the Chinese tomb changed all of that.

What happened in between these two historic events is also a mystery since no other archaeological evidence has been uncovered to precisely document as to why neckcloths were worn.

Was the cloth designed for a special purpose or did it designate the wearer as being special? Was it a status symbol? Thousands of years ago cloth was a precious commodity. Dare it be wasted on a purely ornamental object? It wasn't until the Renaissance that extravagance became a way of life and men outdid themselves wearing clothing made of rich and luxurious fabrics trimmed in gold. Neckwear, at this time, became elaborate as well, until such excessiveness was condemned.

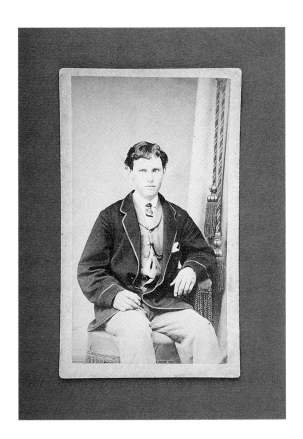

By the 17th century, during the Thirty Years War (1618-1648), neckcloths or cravats worn by Croatian mercenaries were admired by Louis XIII and the French Court. By 1660, the cravat, made mostly of lace, became an adopted way of dress and has been depicted in paintings, prints, and engravings from the mid-17th century onward. From France, the fashion spread to England and then to the American colonies.

By the mid-18th century, long or short cravats accompanied by plain neck bands or pleated stocks was the fashion of the American colonists. Cravats in America were not as fancy or elaborate as those found in Europe. Linen and muslin was used more often than lace. Sometimes the cravat was only trimmed in lace. By the late 1700s, frilly ruffles, later called jabots, were worn with waistcoats. This style continued until around 1840.

George Bryan Brummell, more commonly referred to as Beau Brummell, made a dramatic impression on men's fashion in the 19th century which still holds true today. It had been said that Brummell strived for simplicity, fine lines, neatness, and cleanliness. It was the cravat, and not an ostentatious costume, which Brummell felt should show a man's individuality; thus originated the modern necktie. Brummell insisted that his cravat be arranged, folded, and tied to perfection. It also had to retain its shape without being uncomfortable. Starch was used to create his desired effect and many hours a day were spent trying to create the perfect knot.

Paradoxically, Beau Brummell's high society life was short-lived. Besides being an arrogant sort, Brummell was a gambler with many debts. In 1816, he left England and lived in exile in France in deplorable conditions until his death in an asylum in 1840. By the end of the 19th century, however, Beau Brummell would be remembered as "the Father of Modern Costume."

Many new styles of cravats became fashionable in the 19th century along with old styles which were referred to as "ties." Knotted cravats became increasingly popular while cravats with bows were still used. By the late 19th century, men began to favor knots over bows. The variations of bows and knots became endless and many books were written on the subject. Certain knots were to be worn only by men of specific ages; other knots were favored and worn only by poets, artists, political figures, and celebrities. Some knots were tied tightly while other knots were loosely tied and secured by a stickpin or cravat pin.

Stickpins emerged on the fashion scene around 1830. They were designed with an ornamental top and grooves around the shaft of the pin which kept the stickpin firmly in place. The designs at the top of the stickpin were endless. Anything from a genuine cameo top to precious stones to a whimsical sporting theme became fashionable by the end of the 19th century. Designs were elegant and sometimes elaborate. The vogue for stickpins lasted until the 1920s when tie clasps entered the fashion scene for the modern four-in-hand necktie. Ascots became a fad in the 19th century and they were also held in place by a stickpin.

In 1854, a French photographer named André Adolphe Disderi patented a process whereas images were created on what were called photographic visiting cards (*cartes de visite*). This process allowed all classes of people, not just the wealthy, to have a likeness of themselves created either in a full body pose or a close-up print. Because many were close-ups, the choice of neckwear became crucial. During this period of Queen Victoria's reign, new classes of people were emerging and neckwear was becoming somewhat of a status symbol. Unlike the previous centuries, when neckwear can only observed on paintings and engravings, 19th century costume, and neckwear in particular, can be closely observed by viewing these quaint photographic visiting cards.

At the end of Victoria's reign in 1901, men began to loosen up as far as dress was concerned. This also meant that fewer rules or guidelines were used concerning the correct neckwear to use or the proper knot to tie. The modern day four-in-hand tie began to take precedence over the bow tie at the beginning of the 20th century and is still going strong at the end of the 20th century.

Centuries ago, men's neckwear might have initially been used for functional reasons but today, this useless piece of fabric can be extremely ornamental accentuating the wearer's inner-most desires, feelings, and overall attitudes.

Cover of *"Tie" Talk* from January 1894. Notice the dogs all wearing neckties.

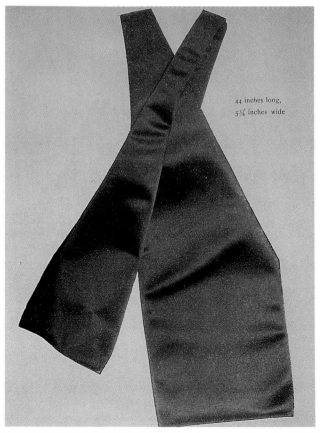

DE JOINVILLE FOUR-IN-HAND Necktie offered for sale in 1896.

FOUR-IN-HAND Necktie offered for sale in 1896 from the Klausner & Company Neckwear Catalogue.

Band & Shield Tecks popular in 1896.

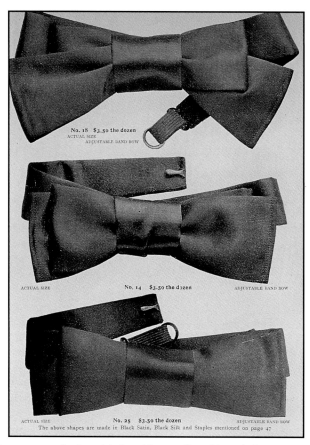

Assortment of adjustable band bows offered for sale in 1896.

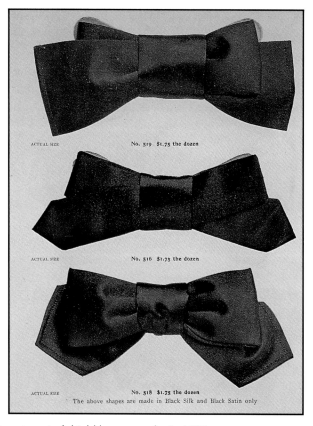

Assortment of shield bows popular in 1896.

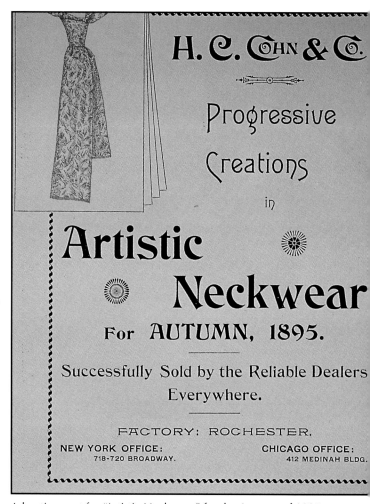

Advertisement for "Artistic Neckwear" for the Autumn of 1895 as featured in *Cloth and Clothing*.

Advertisement for assorted neckwear for the Spring of 1896 as featured in *"Gibson's Clothing Gazette."*

Colorful plaid & striped neck scarfs advertised for sale in 1898 by Bandler Bros. N.Y.

Ad for "The Trueflex" cravat from Rufus Waterhouse Co. New York, 1898.

Trevaskis, *Hazleton, Pa.*

Kellmer, Hazleton, Pa.

Scannell, 814 ARCH STREET, PHILADELPHIA.

S. B. HOFFMEIER,   Easton, Pa.

Chapter I - The First 20 Years

The appearance of the vertical tie known as the four-in-hand tie entered the fashion scene in the second half of the 19th century. Its origin is somewhat sketchy but it had been said that someone knotted his neck scarf in the same manner as the reins of a four-in-hand carriage. This type of knot stayed in place better than the knot of the cravat or even the bow tie. Towards the end of the 19th century when sporting activities of all kinds were in vogue, four-in-hand knots were preferred and more realistic for casual dress associated with some of these activities. Bow ties were still more suited for evening and formal affairs.

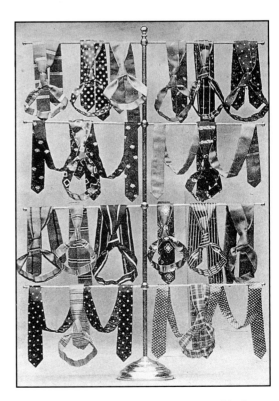

A turn of the century tie display showing reversible four-in-hand neckties.

Assortment of club ties as advertised in the Adolph Levy & Son Neckwear Catalogue from 1902.

Since the art of tying the cravat was indeed just that, an art, some men lacked the confidence they needed to tie the perfect knot. In 1864, the first ready-tied tie was patented but looked down upon by many. However, there was enough men without the confidence needed to tie the perfect knot, making this invention a huge success.

Teck scarfs were advertised widely in 1900. Named after Queen Victoria's cousin, the Duke of Teck, teck scarfs were ready-tied four-in-hand neckties. Made of silk in a large assortment of patterns and colors, they were offered with bands or shields to hold them in place. They were not so well received in the 19th century but their popularity increased in the first decade of the 20th century. The vogue for the teck scarf lasted until about 1930.

During the first decade of the 20th century, four-in-hand ties varied in size as well as in shape. Some ties had pointed bottoms while others had squared bottoms. Most four- in-hand ties, at this time, were 46" or 47" long varying in width from 2" to 2 1/2" wide. Ties measuring 1 1/2" to 1 3/4" wide were referred to as string ties.

During the years associated with World War I (1914-1918), there was not much change or variety in men's neckwear due to war shortages. Dress became less rigid, tie designs were simple. Regimental striped ties became the fashion on both sides of the Atlantic. After the war, tie fabric, and the weave of the fabric as well, became an excellent selling point. Luxurious silks, satins, and brocades were used in abundance. Another important selling point was the length of the band. Ties manufactured by Louis Auerbach & Company in 1918 and 1919 were guaranteed for their superior quality and fine tailoring. Their ties were "made with an extra long slip band, a feature which permits the tie to slide easily through the collar, and eases the strain upon the cravat."

Tie manufacturers used fabric and workmanship as merchandising tools to appeal to men of all income levels. In 1911, an assortment of four-in-hand ties advertised for sale in the Chicago Mail Order catalog were 19 cents each while band tecks were 42 cents each. Higher end haberdashers offered French silk cravats for $5.00 each.

Full dress embroidered bow ties popular in 1902.

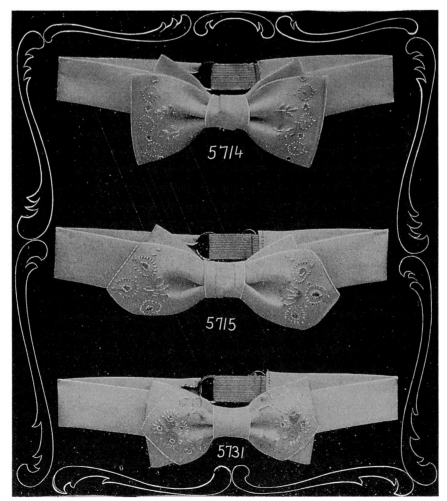

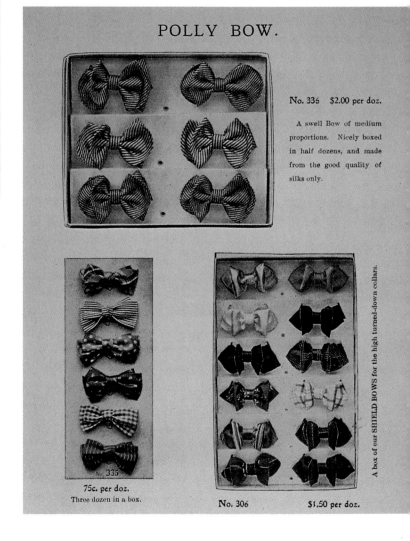

Butterfly & Bat Ties offered for sale in 1902.

Popular styles in bow ties for the 1902 Spring & Summer season.

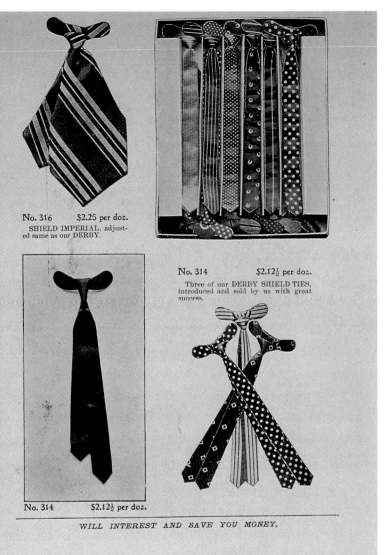

No. 316 $2.25 per doz.
SHIELD IMPERIAL, adjust-
ed same as our DERBY.

No. 314 $2.12½ per doz.
Three of our DERBY SHIELD TIES,
introduced and sold by us with great
success.

No. 314 $2.12½ per doz.

WILL INTEREST AND SAVE YOU MONEY.

Shield Ties popular in 1902 offered from Adolph Levy & Son.

The stylish women of the turn of the century also wore a necktie.

A 1900 Sears, Roebuck & Company advertising page for men's silk neckwear referred to as Teck Scarfs.

This ad from 1909 describes reversible four-in-hand neckties, teck scarfs with band, teck scarfs with shields, all made of silk.

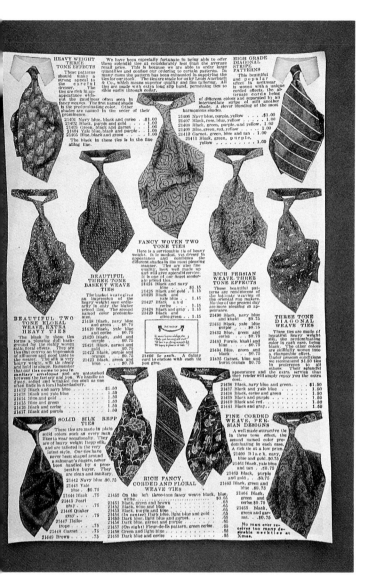

Fancy woven ties in luxurious fabrics offered for sale in 1919 from Baird-North Company.

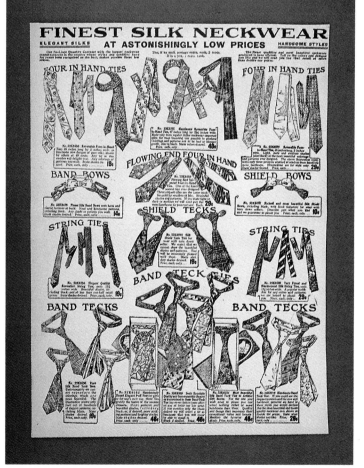

An assortment of men's neckwear advertised for sale in 1908 from Sears, Roebuck & Company.

Chapter II -
The 1920s & 1930s

By the early 1920s, silk was still the most popular choice for tie fabric. Men's neckties advertised in 1922 as being made of heavy silk cost more than those advertised made of rich silk. I wonder what the difference really was! Ties made of a silk and wool combination were advertised as a "favored new fabric so woven that it does not wrinkle."

Knit ties were extremely stylish in the 1920s and they came in all shapes and sizes. Many different color combinations and patterns were offered. There were close knit, loose knit, two-toned knit, lace knit, and even reversible knit ties. Purple, black, brown, navy, wine, and burgundy were fashionable colors of the period.

College striped ties were very common in the 1920s. Usually constructed of silk repp, the school tie was a diagonal stripe geared for the college student who proudly wanted to display his school colors and express his proud affiliation for his particular college or university.

But the most important feature of men's neckwear in the 1920s was resilience. Up until this point, normal tie manufacturers did not solve the problem of preventing the tie from creasing or wrinkling. Certain manufacturers advertised all-wool linings or no stretch stitching for ties to retain their shape after long wear but something was still needed to solve the problem of the short life expectancy of the necktie.

A Charles Williams Store ad for striped knit ties, circa 1925.

Christmas gift giving ideas from A. Sulka & Company, Paris and New York. Notice the price of the French silk cravats. *Harper's Bazaar*, November 1921.

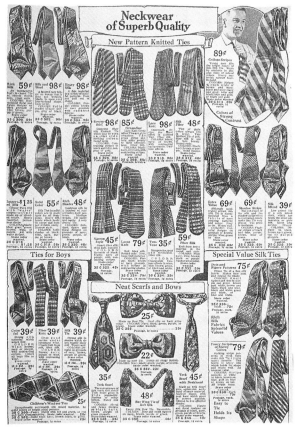

A 1922 Montgomery Ward offering of men's assorted neckwear.

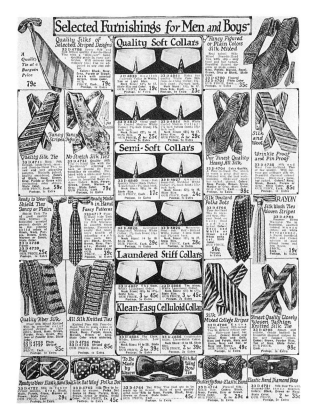

Neckties and bow ties popular in 1925, Charles William Stores.

Men's ties were still referred to as cravats in this 1930s ad from Wilson Brothers Haberdashery.

Colorful assortment of men's neckties in prints and solids offered from Montgomery Ward in 1934.

All Over Patterns

Contrasting Stripes

Neat Figures

44c ea.

Silk Lined

Notice the wide variety
patterns and colors—You
bound to find just the co
and pattern you like!   A
remember—the hand tail
ing and silk lining mea
they'll tie nicely and w
well.   Extraordinary val
even for Wards!
   Pattern Colors: Blue,
o·maroon. State color. Sh
wt. 3 oz.

35 B 1761—Neat figures.
35 B 1762—Allover Patter
35 B 1763—Contrasti
Stripes.
35 B 1760—Square wea
   Solid Colors: na
   blue, royal bl
   maroon, brow
   green or black.
   Each..........

Pebble Grain
Plain Colors

PATTERN A   PATTERN B   PATTERN C   PATTERN D

PATTERN E

WARDS ARE FIRST WITH A REVOLUTIONARY NEW IDEA·
REVERSIBLE SILK TIES—BOTH SIDES ALIKE!
Look Like Regular Ties! Wear Twice as Long Without Cleaning!

No one will know your Tie is reversible except you—for the seam is cleverly hidden at the edges. But if your tie gets soiled or spotted—just wear the other side out—for both sides of these ties are the same! One of those simple ideas you wonder why you didn't think of it yourself! Tailored of excellent quality Weighted silk to knot perfectly, wear splendidly! All Wool bias cut lining prevents wrinkling.

ACTUALLY TWO TIES IN ONE!

95c
2 for $1.85

The patterns have been carefully selected from the newest spring designs.
   Patterns A, B, C and D each in your choice of Blue, Maroon or Brown as shown above. Pattern E, in your choice of Royal, Maroon, Brown, White, Canary, Green or Navy Blue as shown above.
   Be sure to state pattern letter and color wanted in your order. Ship. wt. each 4 oz.; two 7 oz.
35 C 1858—Each 95c; Two for. . $1.85

Reversible silk ties advertised for sale in 1938 from Montgomery Ward.

Checked Moire Stripes

Neat Figured Patterns

9c
ea.
us Fabrics

$1.50 HANDMADE TIES
FOR MEN WHO WANT
STYLE AND QUALITY
$1.00 2 for $1.85

Handmade ties with "New Resilient Construction" advertised for sale in 1937 from Montgomery Ward.

A man by the name of Jesse Langsdorf came up with a solution to the problem. Instead of cutting the tie out of the fabric in an up and down direction, Langsdorf cut diagonally or on the bias of the fabric. This cut added more strength and elasticity to the fabric and allowed the finished tie to drape better and finally to wear longer. The cut was also made in three pieces instead of the original one cut, and the construction of the tie differed also. This process known as Resilient Construction was patented in 1924 by Jesse Langsdorf for his company known as Resilio.

Resilient construction also changed the way fabric for ties was designed. At this time, the designs on the fabric had to be either woven or printed at an angle so that when the cut was made, the appearance of the pattern was not haphazard.

Arrow necktie ad from *Esquire*, January 1937.

Things slowed down temporarily in the tie manufacturing business during the crash on Wall Street in 1929. By the 1930s, however, movie stars in Hollywood as well as the characters they portrayed in the movies became the fascination of Americans. Tie sales boomed once again with millions of Americans trying to emulate their idols of the Silver Screen.

Attention was also focused on Britian's Edward, Prince of Wales, who later became the Duke of Windsor. Edward VIII was a handsome, dignified man who was greatly admired. He became a fashion leader for millions of men on both sides of the Atlantic. His famous Windsor knot for the four-in-hand tie was emulated tremendously from the late 1930s and onward.

The gangster era was also in full swing in this period. These stylish hoodlums wore pin-striped double-breasted suits, striped shirts, colorful ties, and felt hats. Their behavior commanded a wild yet stylish look, unlike the conservative business suit of the period.

Magazine illustration of a fashionable shop off Bond Street in London showing a window display of neckties, *Esquire*, April 1939.

Many services were provided in the 1930s for men to color coordinate their suits with "colors that click." In 1938, Real Silk Hoisery Mills in Indianapolis, Indiana, advertised its service for men to accurately color coordinate their socks, shirt, and ties with their suits. Effective groupings were shown to anyone for the asking. This service was designed to create "color assurance" since many men felt insecure about choosing the proper tie. The McCurrach Organization in New York City offered a similar service. Each McCurrach tie came with "pre-planned color harmony" recommending the exact color suit to wear with each particular tie. This information was found on the tie band.

Distinctive new neckwear patterns began showing up in mail order catalogs and period magazines in the early 1930s. At this time, rayon, sometimes referred to as artificial silk, became one of the most popular fabrics used. Silk repp, satin, and brocade were also fashionable. Stripes, checks, allover patterns, and small prints were very common. Solid color ties were also popular and extremely stylish with striped or solid color shirts.

Van Heusen ad for shirts and ties, *Esquire*, May 1939.

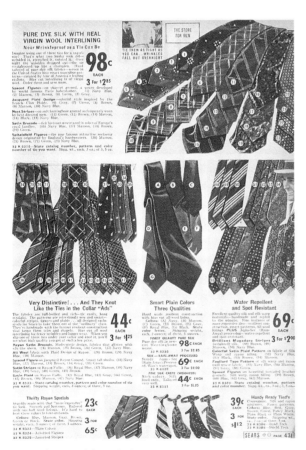

Ties advertised for sale from Sears in 1939.

In 1937, Montgomery Ward offered "Thrift Quality" neckties made of exceptional fabrics with both ends satin faced. These ties sold for twenty-five cents each. Their finest line advertised as "Puppy Skin Ties" were made of DuPont Rayon Mogodore and priced at fifty cents each.

In the late 1930s, the prints on the ties were becoming more elaborate as well as the weave of the fabric with rayon jacquard being extremely desirable at this time. Twill weaves were also popular along with herringbone weaves. Towards the end of the decade, ties were advertised as water repellent, spot resistant, and almost completely wrinkleproof.

Ties and socks made of Congo cloth advertised in *Esquire*, June 1939.

Advertisement for Mark Twain shirts featuring all solid color neckties, October 1939.

How to match one's suits with McCurrach neckties advertised in *Esquire*, November 1938.

Dark brown satin brocade
tie, no label. $5-10

Brown satin brocade tie, label
reads "Tuxcraft DE LUXE by
Tuxedo." $10–20

Blue silk tie with multi-
colored pattern woven in a
diagonal fashion. Label
reads "Carlson Cravats."
$10–15

Blue silk tie with white abstract print,
no label.$8–12

Blue silk tie, label reads "Ardsley Twill, woven by
McCurrach." $8–12

Green tie with woven zig zag pattern labeled
"Eugene Jacobs, Famous for Neckwear." $10–15

Woven tie with small print labeled
"Arrow." $5–10

Woven tie with butterfly design. The label
reads "Selected Fabric, Resilient Construction." $8–12

Rust-colored silk tie with woven design.
$8–12

Green silk tie with jacquard weave and small allover pattern; Grey twill tie labeled "Manhattan Shirt Company"; Blue silk tie with allover pattern labeled "Cheney Cravats." $10–15

Two navy blue brocade ties; the tie with the pinwheel design is labeled "Fashion Row Cravats." $10–20

Identical brocade ties in two different colors labeled "National Shirt Shops." $10–15

Two ties with diagonal weaves in two-toned color combinations labeled "Arrow." $8–12

A trio of three-toned diagonally woven ties made of heavy weight silk. The tie with the building design is labeled "Cheney Cravats." $10–20

Three diagonal striped ties made of silk. The black and white tie is labeled "National Shirt Shops, Coast to Coast." $7–10

Striped tie with fancy woven pattern labeled "Hand Tailored." The green tie with the small print is labeled "Cheney Cravats." $5–10

Three fancy woven silk ties with two- and three-toned color combinations. The tie in the center is labeled "Artistic Hand Tailored, Resilient Construction, Baltimore." $10–20

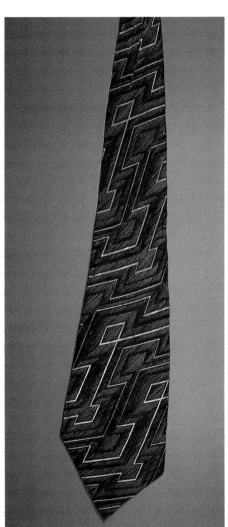

Richly-woven tie with zig zag design, no label. $15–20

Three heavy silk and satin ties with fancy jacquard weaves labeled "Woven by McCurrach." $10–20

Three brocade ties made of silk and rayon taffeta with rich colorings labeled "Arrow" and "Arco." $15–20

Three heavy silk ties with woven floral and butterfly designs, no labels. $15–20

Three ties with spaced figures on brocaded grounds, labeled "J. Shainess & Co., New York" and "Altman Cravats." $8–12

Satiny stripes and jacquard weaves make these three ties very appealing. The blue swirl tie is labeled "by Haband, Rayon." $12–20

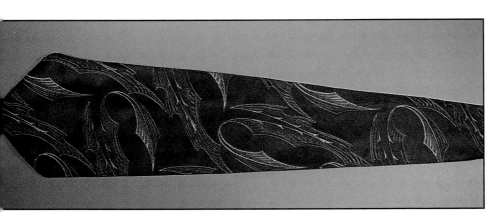

This lovely rayon satin brocade tie with abstract pattern bears no label. $15–20

Two ties with fancy swirl and paisley designs, no labels. $15–20

This rich-colored rayon tie with brocaded leaf design is labeled "Wembley." $15–20

Leaf, floral, and abstract designs were woven into these three early ties. The floral tie is labeled "Morro Cravats." $15–20

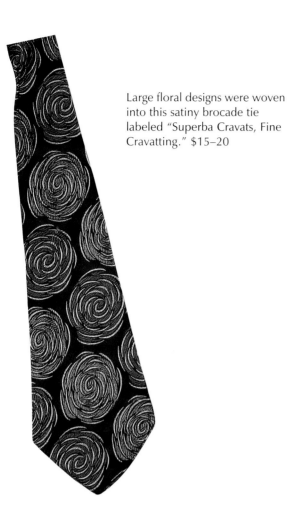

Large floral designs were woven into this satiny brocade tie labeled "Superba Cravats, Fine Cravatting." $15–20

Hand painted rayon taffeta tie which reads "We Want Beer, Bring Back Prosperity." $25–50

This 1920s diagonal striped tie was embellished with floral appliques during the Depression in the 1930s. $10–15

Chapter III -
The War Years 1940-1945

When the Second World War broke out in Europe in 1939, Americans had to cut the apron strings with England and stand on its own. Britain was at a standstill, and enforced clothing rationing began in 1940. Europe's manufacture of neckties was put on hold. At this time, American creativity blossomed and by the time the war had ended, the American tie market flourished.

The Botany Worsted Mills located in Passaic, New Jersey, took out full page ads in men's magazines promoting their wrinkle-proof ties in stripes, plaids, and planned patterns as well as "other patterns" which were beginning to saturate the American market. These other patterns, modeled after the style known as Art Deco which was popular in the 1920s and 1930s, were the beginnings of the bold abstract and geometric ties that took the country by storm after the war.

The Cluett, Peabody & Company, better known as Arrow, also promoted their line of neckties displaying abstract and geometric patterns with new lines introduced each month. In November of 1942, most of the Arrow designs were diagonal stripes, but a year later, Peacock Satins were the newest craze and in 1944 almost all of the patterns were abstract or geometric.

With silk and other fabrics being rationed, Americans turned to rayon for tie manufacturing. Referred to as artificial silk in the past, rayon was a good choice for the new styles in neckties about to emerge.

Planned pattern ties from Botany in fall colors, September 1941.

Ad for The Original French Panel Tie, woven in the U.S. and featured in *Life*, October 1940.

Botany ties in assorted patterns designed to go with summer suits, May 1942.

Fall tie assortment from Arrow, November 1942.

Peacock Satins by Arrow popular in 1943.

The popular feather motif is seen in this tie by Beau Brummell, December 1944.

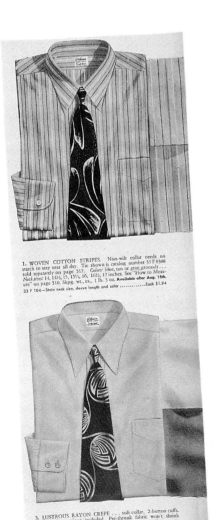

Two abstract ties featured in the Sears Fall & Winter catalog of 1943-44.

Ad for men's leisure suits showing bold tie designs in 1943.

Very loud tie designs were beginning to appear in mail order catalogs by 1944.

Pilgrim ties offered for sale from Sears in 1944 made of assorted rayon fabrics with abstract and geometric designs.

Ad for Regal Ties manufactured by Frank & Meyer Neckwear Company, St. Louis, Missouri, December 1944.

Above:
Pilgrim "Nobility" ties offered for sale from Sears in 1943 featuring resilient construction and the new "full drape" construction which meant that more material was used to make the tie wider giving a "richer looking drape."

Pilgrim "Fashion Tower" economy ties offered for sale from Sears in 1943.

Christmas ad from Botany Ties featuring assorted patterns and fabrics, *Esquire*, December 1944.

Christmas ad from Cohama Ties, *Esquire*, December 1944.

Arrow tie ad featuring their new line of color geometrics.

Ad for foulard ties by Cohama, *Esquire*, March 1943.

Solid color neckties by Superba advertised in December of 1944.

Corded silk tie with three-toned abstract pattern, no label. $10–15

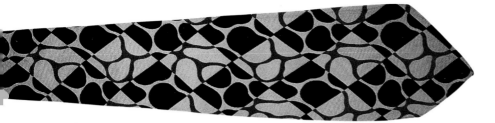

Two wool ties with Persian-style print and allover pattern labeled "Wembley."
$8–12

"Class of 41" tie made of four-toned silk jacquard. $20–30

This unusual tie with embroidered design bears no label. $12–18

Right:
Brown silk moiré tie with feather design labeled "American Game Birds, Cheney Cravats." $15–20

Rayon taffeta tie labeled "Bird Plumage, Cheney Cravats." $15–20

This novelty tie for St. Patrick's Day is made of rayon, labeled "Wilson Faultless, Made in USA." $15–20

Chapter IV -
On The Wild Side 1945-1955

Europe suffered tremendously from the effects of World War II. None of the European countries were in any position to design or manufacture neckties when the war ended. Since America had become independent of Europe when the war started, by the time it was over, the manufacturing of bold neckties was already in full swing. Europe now turned to America for fashion.

The soldiers needed a lift, and bright colors, classy suits, and especially wild neckties fit the bill. Postwar optimism was running rampant. The tie manufacturers, trying to fulfill the need of the returning GIs, resorted the prewar Art Deco style for inspiration, and as a result created some of the most flamboyant neckties in history.

The Art Deco style, consisting of abstract and geometric designs, fit the bill for necktie patterns. Circles, squares, and triangles designed with abstract connotations in bright colors were very desirable. Three dimensional abstract designs were also common, along with anything resembling the Modern Age. Lightening bolts, zig zags, sunrays, and leaping gazelles were fabulous design motifs.

In 1945, McCurrach, a New York City firm, promoted their line of ties called "Verticals." This line of modern ties used complimentary and contrasting color schemes in the patterns which were described as "sharp and severe, to run down your tie instead of on the conventional diagonal." What a difference from the prewar brocades.

Feathers, flowers, and leaves were also common design themes in postwar necktie manufacturing.

"Tropical Bird Plumage," a new line of ties by Cheney Cravats in 1945, consisted of eighteen patterns in six different color combinations with "the distinctive colorings of tropical birds." These ties were made of rayon faille moiré.

Flowers of every type were also displayed on men's neckties in wild color combinations. The flowers were either accurately portrayed or created in the abstract. The same held true for ties with leaf prints.

The vivid color combinations became an important factor in the design of these ties. Many of the inspirations were drawn from Far Eastern and Middle Eastern textiles and prints. In 1947, Manhattan Shirt Company, who also manufactured men's ties, created patterned ties with the designs taken from "rare old Chinese screens." In the same year, Arrow created their "Bagdad Motifs" which were advertised to "whisk your memories back to the marvelous land of Sinbad the Sailor." Other designs in this line were "Magic Coins...Ali Baba's Sword...the Caliph's Castle...the Genie... the Veil of Arabia and other motifs from the Arabian Nights."

Using exotic places for necktie design became increasingly popular. One of the most desirable types of the exotic tie lines were those which depicted palm trees and flamingos. These exotic features were usually either printed on the fabric, silk-screened, hand painted, or actual photographs were used and processed onto the tie fabric, new technology in 1947.

Men who enjoyed the outdoors were particularly fond of wildlife motifs. Gamebirds, hunting dogs, deer, sailfish, sailboats, and lake and mountain scenes were some of the popular themes. It was not hunting dogs alone that were portrayed, but any breed of man's best friend was woven, silk-screened, hand painted, or printed on a necktie.

Western themes were extremely common on men's neckties. Inspiration was drawn from the Old West in addition to what was portrayed in Hollywood, with idols like Roy Rogers and Hopalong Cassidy. Early television westerns also provided more impetus for the western look on ties as well as clothing for men and boys.

In 1944, Manhattan Ties advertised their line of ties called "Frontier Prints." This line included "Patterns of the Old Frontier with its rugged, masculine beauty...Covered Wagon...Iron Horse...Spurs...Wagon Wheel...Longhorn...Ten Gallon Hat and Lariat."

Horses, in particular, were featured on men's ties and some were hand painted by Western artists and at the time sold for quite a bit of money. Ties painted by a commercial artist named Til Goodan are extremely collectible today. Rodeo themes, bucking broncos, campfires, steer heads, and desert cactus were other popular motifs.

The hand painting of ties, in general, became common practice in the 1940s. Individual artists began the practice after World War II and as popularity increased the major tie manufacturers jumped on the band wagon using either famous or infamous artists to create unusual designs. Besides the western themes, other novelty motifs were hand painted on ties including the great outdoors, palm trees and flamingos, animals, flowers, feathers and leaves, pin-ups, hula and exotic dancers, and advertising gimmicks to name just a few. Artistic ties were individualized and personalized. They became the focus of tie collections in the late 1940s and early 1950s, and are among the most desirable examples today. Besides the actual hand painting, many of the ties were silk-screened and occasionally air-brushed.

Going one step further, the ties designed and painted by famous artists are the cream of the crop. The top of the list includes ties hand painted by surrealistic artist Salvador Dali. Although certain designs created by Dali had to be reworked because of their graphic nature, most of his designs include the abstract surrealism he is noted for. Each Dali tie was signed on the front, titled, and given a name which could be found on the back of the tie. Labels varied since Dali was con-

tracted by several manufacturers. It is not actually known how many different ties were designed and painted by Dali, although one contemporary New York tie collector boasts that he has seventy-five Salvador Dali neckties.

Second on the list were the ties designed by Countess Mara, an Italian born designer. Produced in limited quantity, her designs were all quite appealing, unusual, and pricey at the time. Her initials can be found on the front of the tie, sometimes lost in the actual design; labels bearing her name are found on the back of the tie.

This new found medium for artists and fashion designers to express themselves opened a whole new realm of possibilities and the idea spread to many other women designers in the postwar era. Ties signed Schiaparelli are also desirable as well as those by Tina Lesser. In the 1950s, designer Lilly Daché attached her name to men's ties also.

Two other novelty-type ties which were popular in the postwar era were "girlie" ties and "peek-a-boo" ties. Nudes, exotic dancers, and bathing beauties were the popular motifs for the girlie ties. Most of the designs were hand painted or screen printed. Some girlie ties were also used as advertising gimmicks; the manufacturers knew that their products would sell this way! Peek-a-boo ties, on the other hand, could be worn by a conservative business type since the tie itself was usually a normal looking stripe or planned pattern. It was the lining of the four-in-hand necktie which displayed either a celebrity, a bathing beauty, or an actual nude from a photograph which was processed onto the fabric. The poses of the women were similar to what was found on men's calendars of the period. Many of the peek-a-boo ties have been discarded over the years due to the fact that the surprise that lied within the folds of the necktie were not visible to the average person. Because of this, these ties are extremely collectible today.

Photographic fabrics were introduced in 1947 creating a real sensation in the textile printing industry. Two different processes were used by two different companies. Leize, Inc. of New York used the "Foto-Fab" process using negative film to produce a positive print on fabric while the Ross-Smith Corp. of New York used positive film. Dresses, blouses, pillows, and neckties were adorned with actual photographs of people, places, and things.

Abstract & Geometric

Grey and salmon-colored tie with circle design. The paper tie band reads "Quality Cravat, Resilient Construction, For Men Who Discriminate." $18–25

Two silk ties and one rayon tie with circular patterns labeled "Arrow" and "Park Lane." $18–25

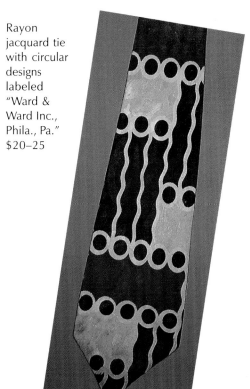

Rayon jacquard tie with circular designs labeled "Ward & Ward Inc., Phila., Pa." $20–25

Three rayon ties with circular patterns labeled "Classic Tru Val Original" and "Beau Brummell." $20–30

"Verticals," a fashion first from McCurrach; ties with "sharp, severe patterns to run down your tie instead of on the conventional diagonal," circa 1945.

Two ties, one of silk and the other of rayon, both with circular patterns labeled "Manhattan" and "Beau Brummell." $20–30

Beau Brummell ties advertised in *Life* Magazine, March 1947.

The diagonal striped repp tie is labeled "A Van Heusen Original"; the rayon tie with circle designs is not labeled. $20–25

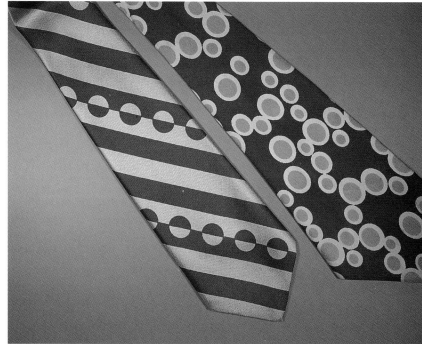

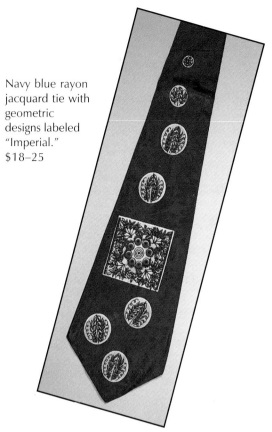

Navy blue rayon jacquard tie with geometric designs labeled "Imperial." $18–25

Brown rayon jacquard tie with circular patterns. The store label reads "Keller's Men's Shops, Phila., Pa." $25–30

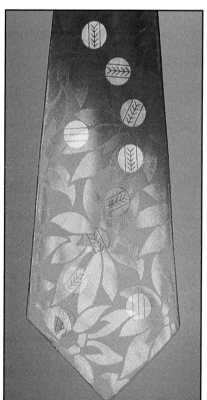

The color in this rayon jacquard tie fades from deep burgundy to almost yellow, no label. $25–30

A waffled fabric was used to create these two bold neckties, no labels. $25–30

Rust-colored rayon jacquard tie with circular patterns labeled "Beau Brummell." $22–28

Pilgrim ties advertised for sale from Sears in 1946. All ties were wool interlined and made of luxurious fabrics with abstracts, geometrics, solids, checks, plaids, and planned patterns.

Two wide rayon ties with circular patterns labeled "Arrow" and "Morro Custom Cravats." $25–30

Two rayon ties with circle designs labeled "Towncraft De Luxe Cravat, Resilient Construction, Fabric Loomed in USA." $25–30

Two ties, one of rayon jacquard and the other of silk repp, both with geometric designs labeled "Styled by Green Valley." $25–30

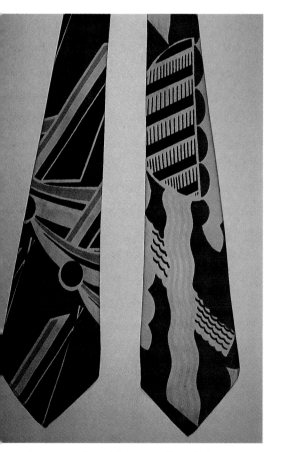

Two rayon ties with geometric and abstract designs, both utilizing the same color combinations labeled "Wilson Brothers Duratwill, A Rayon fabric of Celanese Yarn" with a store label which reads "Boardwalk Tie Shop, Atlantic City, New Jersey." $22–28

Two geometric ties in yellow and blue labeled "Regal Cravat." $22–30

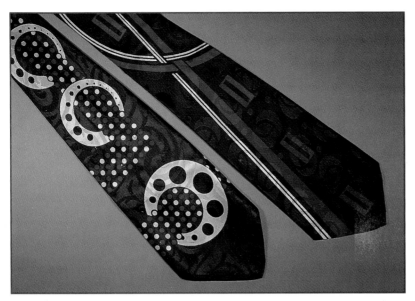

Two rayon jacquard ties with geometric designs labeled
"Croydon Cravats" and "Kreway." $20–30

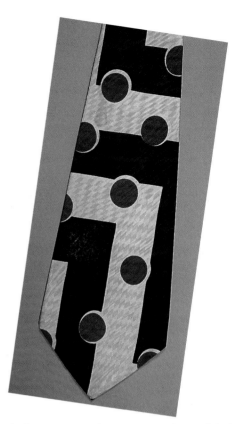

Tie made of silk grosgrain with geometric print, no label.
$20–25

Van Heusen ties advertised in 1947.

Olive green rayon jacquard tie with geometric print, no label.
$20–25

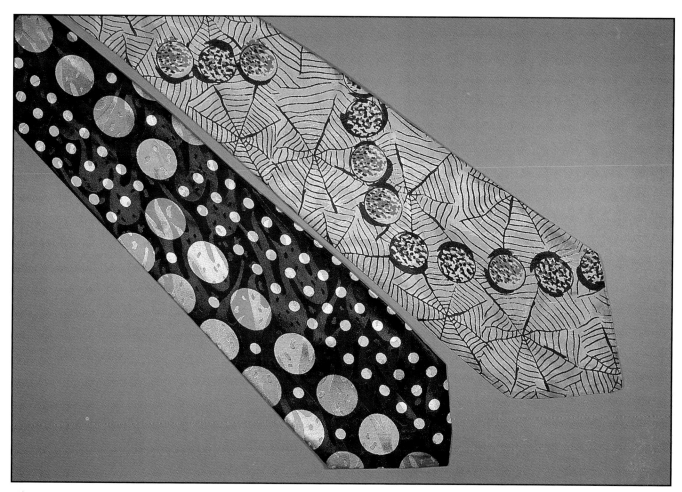

Silk tie with spider web design labeled "An Original by Damon"; black rayon jacquard tie with pink, white and grey polka dots labeled "Norman Samm Original." $20–30

Two rayon jacquard ties with feather and leaf designs labeled "Haband." $20–30

Two rayon ties with circle designs. The navy tie is labeled "Van Heusen Original, Van Splendor." $22–28

Two rayon jacquard ties with circle patterns. The wine-colored tie is labeled "Bond Style Manor." $20–30

Abstract and geometric patterns decorate these two rayon ties labeled "Croydon Cravats." $20–25

Concentric circles, polka dots, and paisley prints decorate these three rayon ties labeled "A Jon Coro Exclusive" and "Londonderry Cravat." $18–25

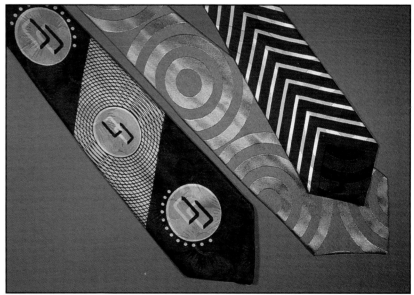

Two rayon jacquard ties with geometric prints labeled "Original by Damon." $20–25

Wembley ties advertised in 1947.

Navy blue rayon tie with abstract floral pattern labeled "Smoothie Imperial." $18–22

Geometric print tie in brown rayon jacquard labeled "Beau Brummell." $20–25

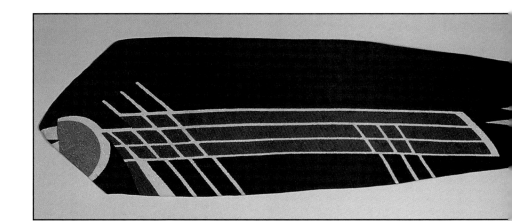

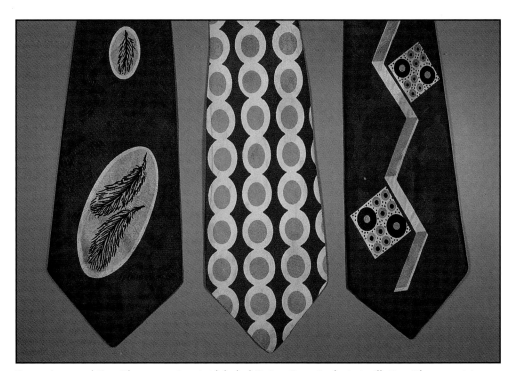

Rayon jacquard tie with geometric print labeled "A Jon Coro Exclusive; silk tie with geometric print labeled "An Original by Damon"; feather design on burgundy rayon jacquard labeled "Original Van Heusen." $18–22

Burgundy rayon jacquard tie with geometric print originally purchased at "Radio City Neckwear, House of Neckties, New York City." $20–25

Brown rayon tie with geometric print labeled "A Van Heusen Original." The rayon jacquard tie with three-dimensional pattern is labeled "An Empeeco Cravat." $20–25

Tie with Persian print on rust-colored rayon jacquard labeled "Haband, One of a Kind Series"; tie with geometric print is labeled "ARTcrest, The Best." $20–25

Left: Silk tie with geometric print, tie band reads "Morro Custom Cravats, Wrinkle Resistant, 100% wool-lined, As Advertised in *Esquire*." Right: Geometric print tie on rayon jacquard labeled "ARTcrest, The Best." $20–25

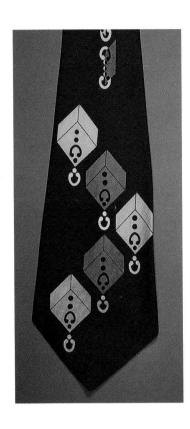

Burgundy tie with three-dimensional geometric print labeled "Original Van Heusen, Van Cruise." $20–25

Three-toned rayon tie with geometric print labeled "Ward & Ward, Famous for Neckwear." $18–22

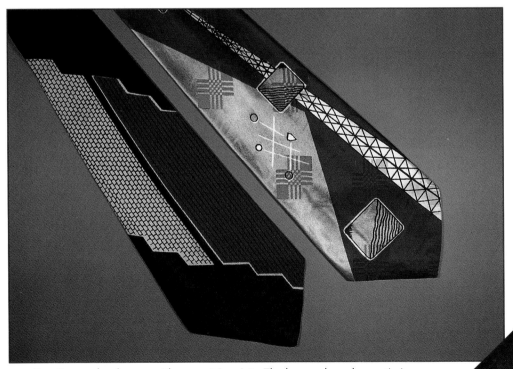

Two ties made of rayon with geometric prints. The burgundy and navy tie is labeled "Van Heusen Original, Van Splendor." $18–25

This brown rayon tie with pink and grey squares bears no label. $20–25

Top: Rayon tie with geometric print labeled "Kent Tie Bar, Philadelphia, Pa., Hand Made." Bottom: Four-toned rayon jacquard tie labeled "Beau Brummell." $15–22

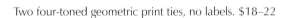

Two four-toned geometric print ties, no labels. $18–22

Two navy blue ties, one of silk, the other of rayon, with abstract and geometric prints labeled "Manhattan, Pure Silk" and "Answorth, New York." $18–22

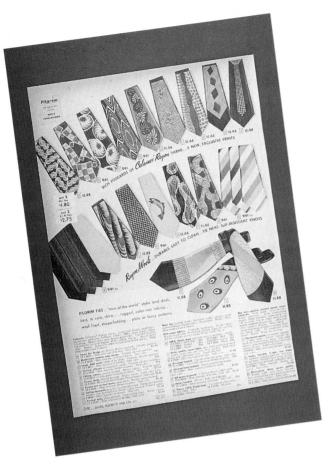

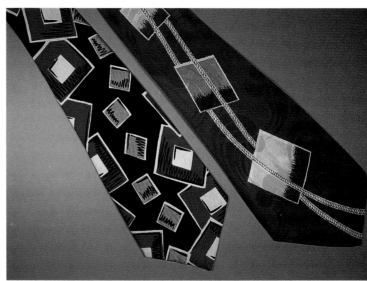

Two rayon ties with bold geometric designs labeled "Regal" and "Arrow." $18–22

Pilgrim neckties offered for sale from Sears in 1949.

Two rayon ties with abstract and geometric prints in shades of brown and purple labeled "Ty Mode Cravats." $20–25

Two ties, one made of silk and the other of rayon, both using four colors in their designs, no labels. $18–22

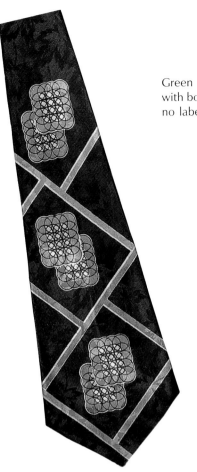

Green rayon jacquard tie
with bold geometric design,
no label. $18–22

Three striking ties with geometric prints, the brown tie is labeled
"Arrow." $18–22

Two brown rayon jacquard ties with geometric
prints labeled "Panels King Size, Resilient
Construction" and "Van Heusen Original." $18–
22

Holiday ad from Arrow featuring "Carol Tones" shirts, ties, and
handkerchiefs, January 1949.

Two rayon ties with abstract and geometric prints labeled "Towncraft De Luxe, Fabric Loomed in USA." $18–25

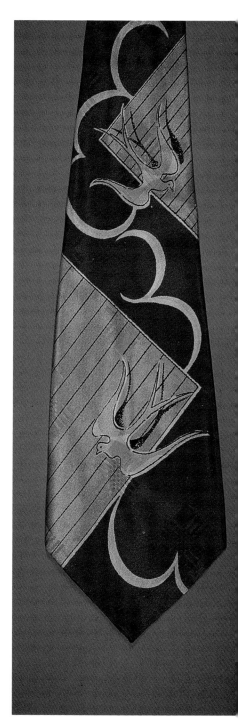

Rayon jacquard tie with bird design labeled "Green Valley Cravat." $22–28

Two silk ties with geometric prints. The burgundy tie is labeled "Jarnac, All Silk, Resilio." $20–25

Two- and three-toned rayon ties with abstract and geometric prints labeled "Van Heusen, Van Cruise." $18–25

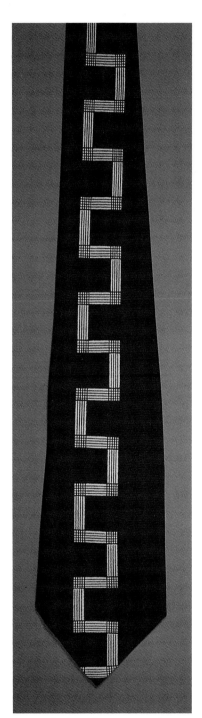

Burgundy tie with geometric design, no label. $18–22

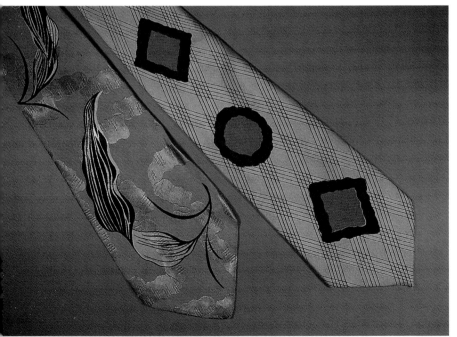

Silk tie with geometric print and rayon jacquard tie with leaf design, both no labels. $20–25

Panel tie offered from Sears in 1949.

Burgundy rayon tie with triangles within triangles labeled "Van Heusen Original, Van Cruise." $17–20

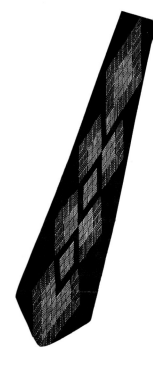

More triangle designs are found on this rayon twill tie labeled "Wilson Faultless, Made in USA." $17–20

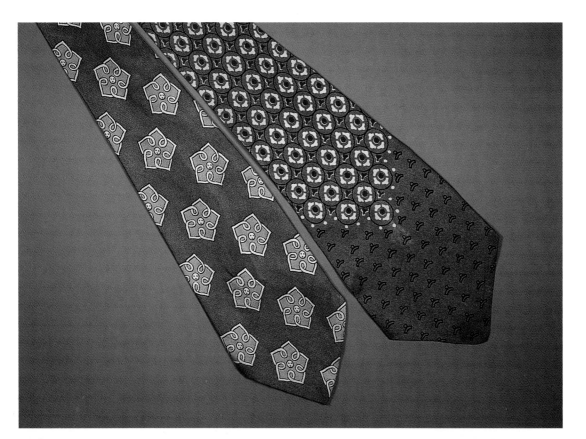

Two lavender rayon ties with geometric prints, no labels. $15–20

Native American-style prints are found on these two rayon ties labeled "Brent" and "Tepee Stripes, Ties by Walker." $18–22

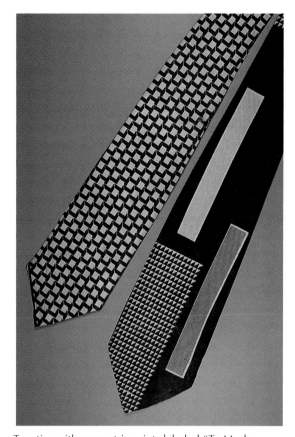

Two ties with geometric prints labeled "Ty-Mode Cravats" and "Manhattan Shirt Co." $15–18

Two three-toned rayon jacquard ties with geometric prints labeled "Pilgrim Cravats." $18–22

Dress and casual ties from Wembley, *Esquire*, 1952.

Two tri-color rayon ties with abstract and geometric designs labeled "Arrow" and "Ward & Ward." $20–25

Two tri-color rayon ties with abstract prints, no labels. $18–22.

"Lucky Ties" by Regal, manufactured by Frank & Meyer Neckwear Company, circa 1952.

Two rayon jacquard ties with abstract and geometric prints, no labels.
$20–25

Two burgundy rayon ties with geometric prints labeled
"Arco Royal." $18–22

Three four-toned rayon ties with geometric prints labeled "Arrow" and
"Leeds." $18–22

Two identical rayon ties made with different color combinations, no labels. $12–18

Two rayon ties for boys with patterns just like Dad's, labeled "Oxford Boy's Tie, Spruce Cravats." $10–15

A tri-colored diamond pattern takes center stage on this rayon tie labeled "Diplomat." $18–22

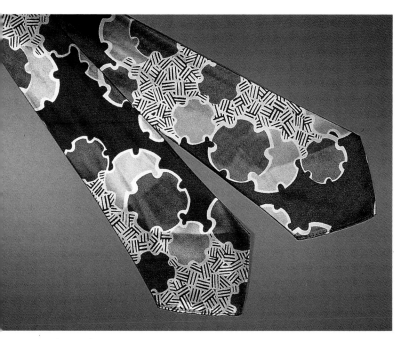

Two identical rayon ties for boys in different color combinations labeled "Oxford Boy's Tie, Spruce Cravats." $10–15

Four-toned rayon tie with abstract print, no label. $18–22

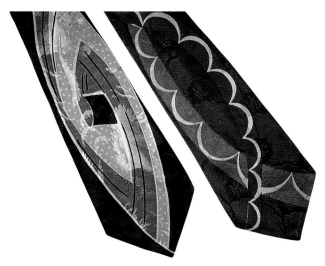

Two four-toned rayon jacquard ties; the tie with the red arc is labeled "Sir by Botany." $20–25

Top: Silk tie with abstract pattern in brown and rust tones labeled "Made for Realsilk, All Pure Silk." Bottom: Abstract print tie made of pure silk; store label reads "Wm. H. Wanamaker, Chestnut St., Phila." $18–22

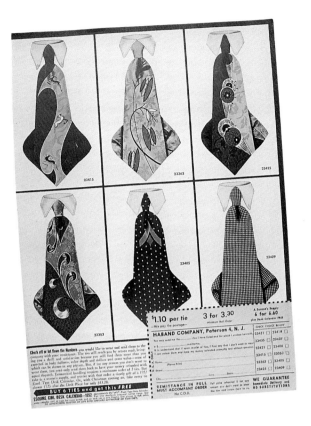

Wild and wonderful ties offered for sale from Haband in 1951.

Two rayon ties with abstract and geometric designs labeled "Melmar" and "Yankee Cravat." $20–25

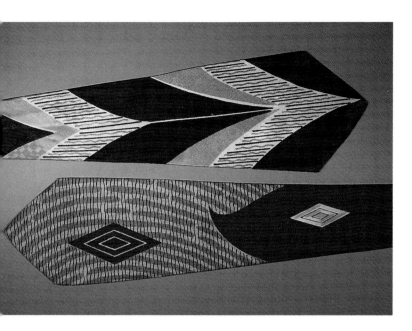

Burgundy and grey v-striped rayon tie labeled "Palm Creation - the talk of the nation." Silk tie with red and grey diamond pattern labeled "Hand Tailored Brae-Mawr cravated, Imported Silk." $20–25

Two 5-inch wide ties with colorful bold patterns labeled "Bond Style Manor" and "Diplomat Ties." $18–22

Three rayon ties with unusual prints labeled "Arco Chukker Crepe" and "Burma." $18–22

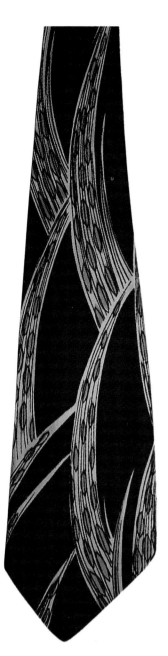

Three-toned silk tie with
abstract design labeled
"Cohama California
Swagger." $15–20

Rayon jacquard tie with spider
web design, no label. $20–30

Rayon tie with swirl design labeled
"London Cravat, Made in USA."
$18–22

A ribbon-like design
runs up and down this
half plain and half
checked tie; store label
reads "P. Deisroth's
Sons, Hazleton, Pa."
$15–20

Rayon tie with yellow and burgundy swirl design labeled "Smoothie Imperial."
Burgundy rayon tie with abstract flower print, no label. $18–22

Two identical ties in different color combinations, five inches wide, labeled
"Paneled Fashion, Resilient Construction." $20–25

Grey rayon jacquard tie with abstract
floral design in black, white, and red,
no label. $18–22

Three-toned rayon tie with swirl
design labeled "Panel Modes,"
manufactured by Randa Neckwear
Corp., Hackensack, New Jersey.
$18–22

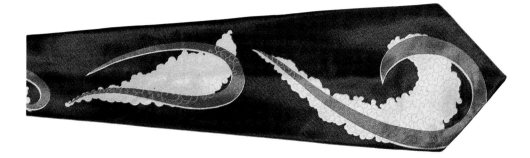

Abstract and geometric tie assortment offered from Wembley in 1950.

Two ties with abstract patterns both using the same color scheme, no labels. $22–28

Three rayon jacquard ties with abstract designs labeled "Panel Cravat," "Panels King Size Resilient," and "Superba Cravats." $20–25

Silk tie with four-toned abstract pattern labeled "Confined Design, Pure Silk." $22–30

Two ties with abstract prints made of rayon jacquard, no labels.
$18–28

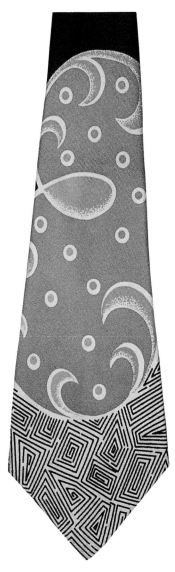

Bright-colored rayon tie with abstract
print, no label. $22 -25

Rayon and silk ties with balloon and ribbon patterns labeled
"Pilgrim Cravats" and "Trojan, Loomed in USA." $22–28

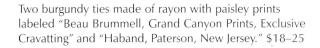

Two burgundy ties made of rayon with paisley prints
labeled "Beau Brummell, Grand Canyon Prints, Exclusive
Cravatting" and "Haband, Paterson, New Jersey." $18–25

Left:
Abstract and three-dimensional summer ties by Wembley, circa 1951.

Right:
Four-toned rayon tie with abstract leaf pattern, no label. $20–25

Two rayon ties with similar design themes labeled "Manhattan Shirt Co." and "Seneca Cravats." $20–25

Monogrammed tie and abstract patterned
tie made of rayon jacquard, no labels.
$20–25

Two rayon ties with ribbon and stylized leaf design labeled "Cohama
California Swagger." $18–22

Two abstract ties made of rayon
jacquard labeled "Ward & Ward,
Famous for Neckwear." $20–25

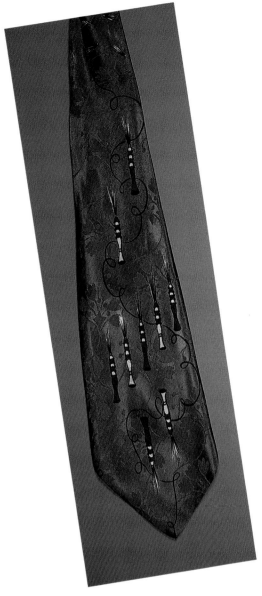

Lavender rayon jacquard tie with abstract
pattern, no label. $15–20

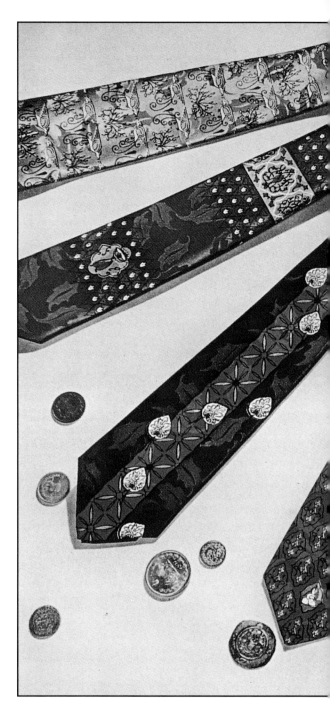

Persian print ties in luxurious rayon jacquard offered for
sale in 1953 by Arrow.

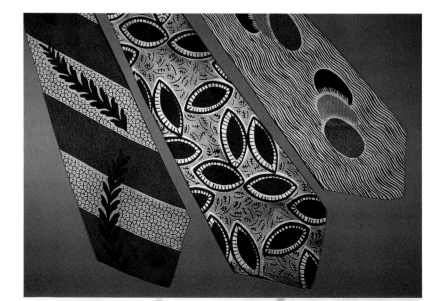

Three rayon ties with abstract patterns; the tie with
the leaf print is labeled "Towncraft De Luxe Cravat."
$18–25

Two four-toned ties with bold allover patterns, no labels. $22–28

Two rayon jacquard ties with geometric and floral designs labeled "Cades - Nothing - But Neckwear, Phila. and Atlantic City" and "Boardwalk Tie Shop, Atlantic City, N.J." $22–28

Geometric print tie made of rayon labeled "Superba Cravats"; silk tie with leaf print, no label. $18–22

Five-toned rayon jacquard tie with abstract print labeled "Sir by Botany." $20–25

Three ties made of silk and rayon with circular and spiral patterns labeled "Arrow" and "Park Lane." $18–22

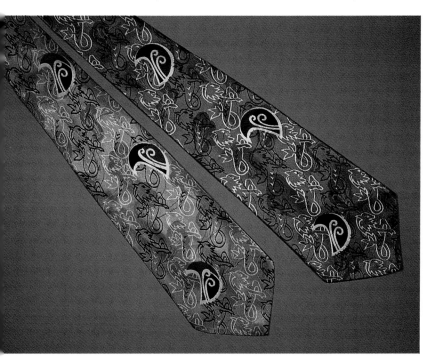

Two identical ties in different color combinations made of rayon jacquard titled "Sea Lion." $15–20

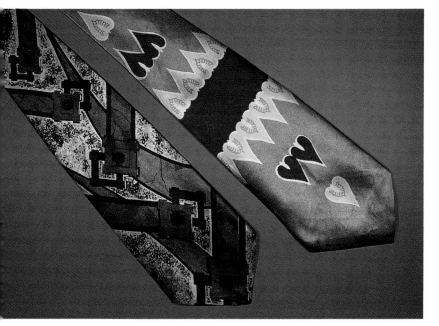

Multi-colored ribbed rayon tie with circular patterns, no label. $20–25

Two rayon ties with abstract and three-dimensional patterns, no labels. $20–25

Burgundy and gold rayon tie with boomer-ang-like design, no label. $22–28

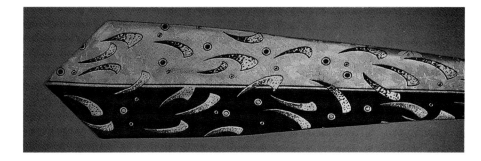

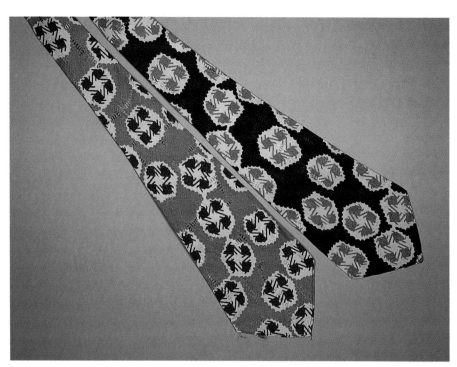

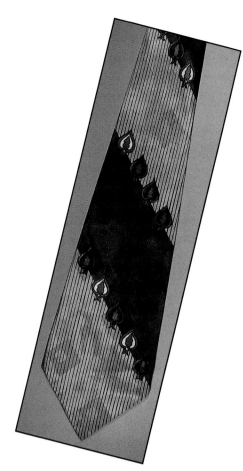

These two rayon ties for boys have an identical pattern but because of the different color combinations, the ties look different. The paper tie band reads "Varsity Campus Styles." $12–15

Rayon jacquard tie with embellished diagonal stripes, no label. $18–22

Silk repp tie with Egyptian print labeled "Haband." Rust-colored silk tie with small spiral designs labeled "Cohama California Swagger." $18–25

Artist Originals by Cutter, October 1953.

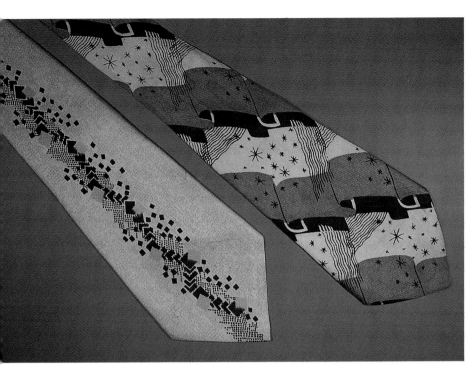

Two rayon ties with three-dimensional prints labeled "Towncraft De Luxe Cravats." $18–25

Artist Originals by Cutter, October 1954.

Abstract tie with honeycomb pattern labeled "Wilshire, Selected Fabric, Resilient Construction." $18–22

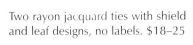

Two rayon jacquard ties with shield and leaf designs, no labels. $18–25

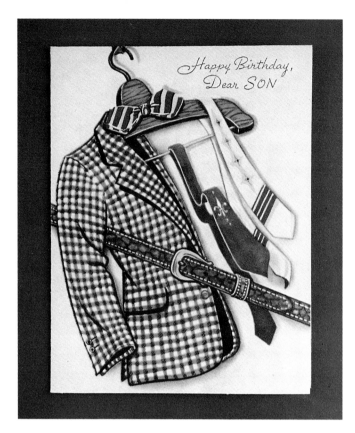

Men's gift giving ideas graphically displayed on this 1950s greeting card.

Two rayon ties with leaf and flower prints labeled "Towncraft De Luxe, Fabric Loomed in USA." $16–20

Silk tie with three-dimensional print labeled "Manhattan." $18–22

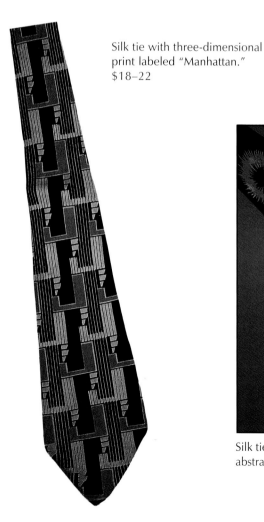

Silk tie with stylized print labeled "Algerian Prints, Crepe Foulard"; silk tie with abstract print, no label. $20–25

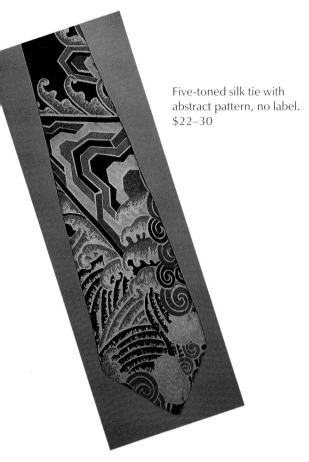

Five-toned silk tie with abstract pattern, no label. $22–30

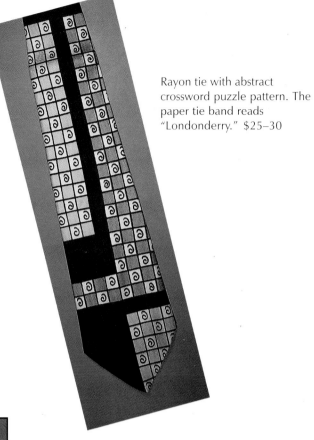

Rayon tie with abstract crossword puzzle pattern. The paper tie band reads "Londonderry." $25–30

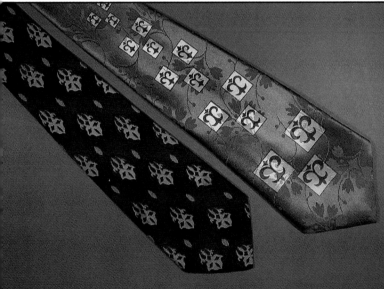

Rayon jacquard tie with *fleur de lis* pattern by "Haband." Burgundy tie with abstract allover pattern labeled "Arrow, All Silk." $18–22

Two three-toned silk ties with bold allover patterns labeled "Superba Cravats." $18–22

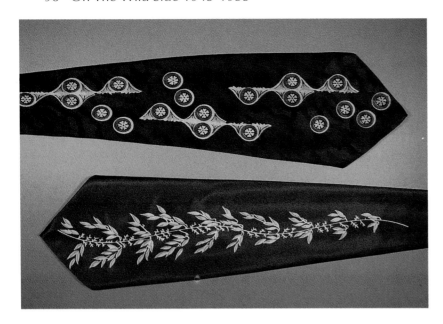

Circle designs and leaf prints are found on these two rayon ties, no labels. $18–22

Three- and four-toned rayon and silk ties with abstract prints labeled "Roselle's, New Brunswick, New Jersey" and "Made Expressly for John Wanamaker." $18–22

Three ties with navy blue backgrounds and abstract prints labeled "A Van Heusen Original" and "Radio City Neckwear, House of Neckties." $18–22

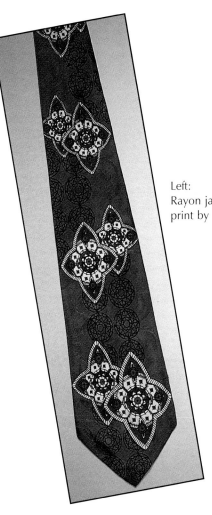

Left:
Rayon jacquard tie with Persian print by "Arrow." $18–22

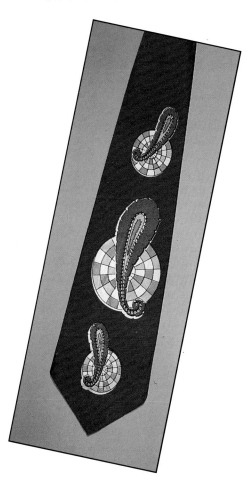

Right
This paisley print tie on rayon jacquard bears no label. $18–22

Rayon tie with three-dimensional print by "Wembley." $25–30

"Falling Leaf Colors…" by Wembley, October 1954

Feathers, Flowers, and Leaves

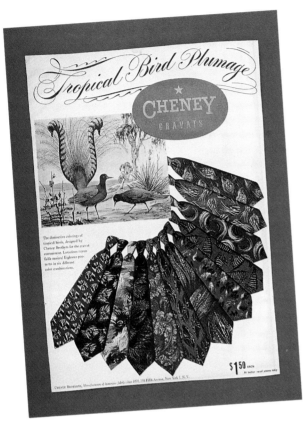

"Tropical Bird Plumage" designed by Cheney Brothers and advertised in April of 1945.

Rayon jacquard tie with large plume design on a diagonal stripe labeled "Arco Royal." $18–22

Feather print tie made of rayon, no label. $18–22

Similar colors were used on these two ties displaying feathers and plumes labeled "Beau Brummell." $20–25

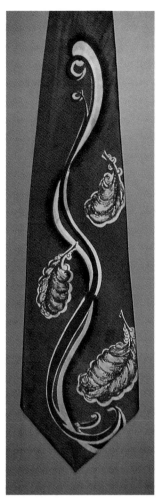

Olive green tie with falling feather design labeled "Richman Brothers." $20–25

Rayon tie with bird and feather design marked "Fiesta" on the back. $20–25

Navy blue satin tie with large paisley print, no label. $18–22

Silk tie with feather-like design, no label. $22–25

Two ties made of virgin wool with leaf and feather designs. The tie with the leaf design is labeled "Botany Regence." $18–25

Navy blue rayon tie with
feather design labeled "The
Imperial by Beau Geste."
$18–22

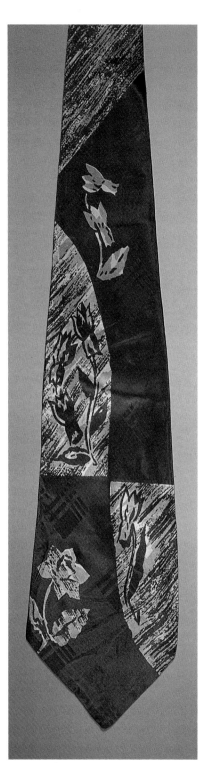

Four-toned rayon jacquard tie with
abstract floral theme, no label. $18–22

Four-toned abstract floral designed tie
labeled "Boardwalk Tie Shop." $18–24

Satin tie with abstract floral design labeled
"Seneca Cravats." $18–22

Two colorful ties with bold floral and bow patterns labeled "Mardi-Gras Prints by Arco" and "Superba Cravats." $22–25

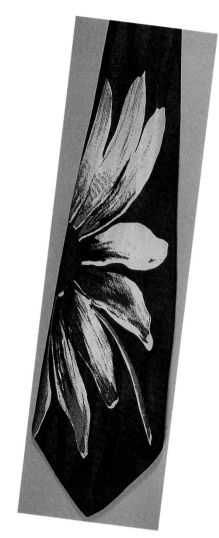

Very artistic silk tie with half of a flower designed as the focal point, no label. $25–30

Rayon tie with four-toned floral print, no label. Geometric tie made of four-toned rayon jacquard labeled "Pilgrim Cravats." $20–25

Hand painted silk tie with leaf and flower design. The label reads "A Work of Art by Di Aljale." $25–30

Two ties with floral and geometric prints made of rayon jacquard labeled "Boardwalk Tie Shop" and "Ward & Ward." $20–25

Rayon jacquard tie with four-toned floral print labeled "Beau Brummell." $20–25

Burgundy rayon tie with red, white, and blue floral design; the store label reads "Scranton Dry Goods Co., Scranton, Pa." Navy blue silk tie with floral design labeled "Carlson Cravats." $18–22

Four-toned rayon tie with floral print, no label. $16–20

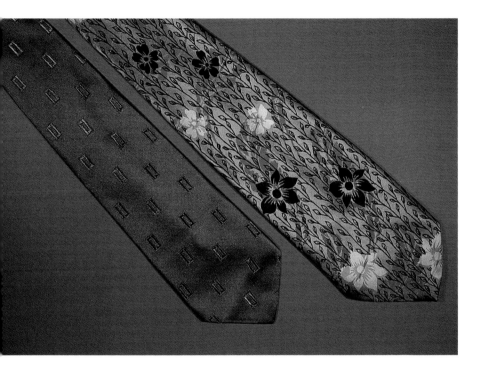

Chartreuse rayon tie with black and white floral pattern, no label. Olive green tie with embroidered geometric design labeled "Imperial Fabric by Resisto." $15–20

Rayon tie with abstract floral design labeled "Coronet Creations." $18–22

Rayon jacquard tie with abstract print; store label reads "Samters of Scranton." $16–20

Rayon tie with leaf design labeled "Pilgrim Cravats in a rayon fabric of Celanese Yarn." $18–22

Green rayon tie with abstract floral print. The tie band reads "Meccador Ties - Extra long to tie a regular or Windsor Knot, All wool lined." $18–22

Rayon tie with abstract floral design. The tie band reads "Morro Custom Cravats, wrinkle resistant, 100% wool lined, as advertised in *Esquire*." $18–22

Two ties, one of silk and the other of rayon, both with floral designs labeled "Arrow." $20–25

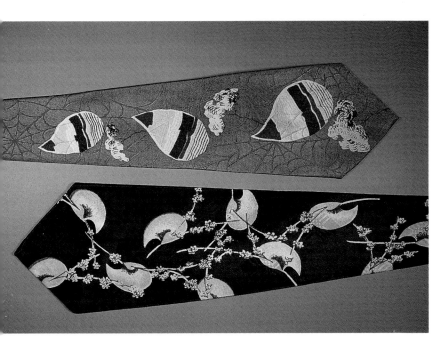

Two abstract ties made of rayon; the lavender tie is labeled "Wembley." $20–25

Two identical ties in different color combinations labeled "Ward & Ward." $20–25

Two rayon ties with abstract designs; the tie with the solid background is titled "Paisley Hearts." $18–22

Burgundy and grey rayon tie with leaf design labeled "Color Symphony, Designed in Paris, Pilgrim Cravats." $20–25

Rayon jacquard tie with floral design in brown and beige tones labeled "by Haband." Chocolate brown silk tie with a large carnation as the focal point labeled "by Haband." $20–25

Two rayon ties with busy backgrounds and small floral prints labeled "Kreway" and "Sidleigh." $16–20

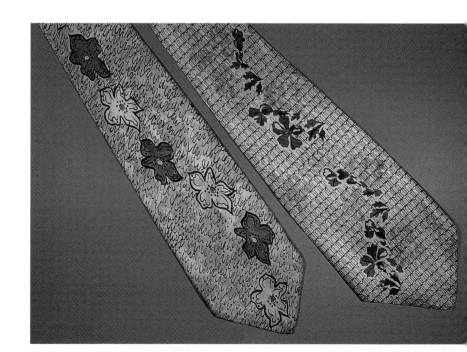

Rayon jacquard tie with floral print labeled "An Empeeco Cravat." $18–22

Brown rayon tie with leaf and flower design labeled "Sir by Botany." Royal blue tie with hand painted leaf design by "Haband." $22–28

Two rayon ties with neat floral prints; the burgundy tie is labeled "Yankee Cravat, SUPER-MADE." $22–28

Grey silk tie with floral design labeled "V. Galét Originals, Beverly Hills, California." $20–25

Two rayon ties with leaf designs labeled "Coast to Coast, National Shirt Shops." $18–22

Two red, white, and blue rayon ties with leaf and flower designs labeled "Howard." $18–22

Yellow tie with hand painted floral design; the tie band reads "Park Avenue Cravats worn by Discriminating Men." $22–28

Two rayon ties designed in Autumn colors with falling leaves labeled "by Haband." $20–25

Two rayon ties with leaf designs in shades of brown, beige, and rust labeled "by Haband" and "Fashion Row Cravats." $18–22

Three-toned rayon tie with leaf print labeled "Broadstreet's, New York, Chicago." $18–22

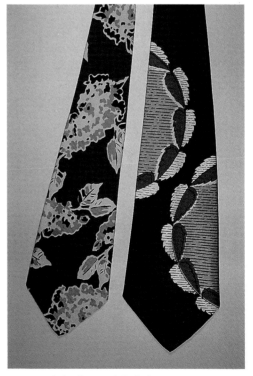

Two rayon ties with leaf prints labeled "Morro Custom Cravats" and "Superba Cravats, The Matterhorn." $18–22

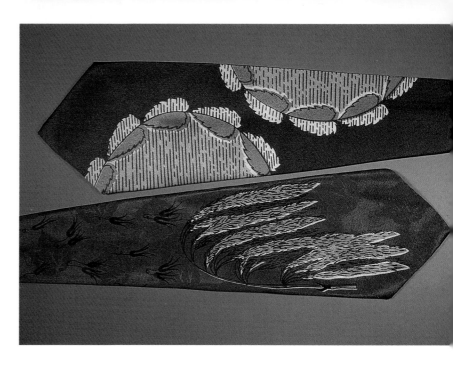

Two brown rayon ties with leaf designs labeled "Morro Custom Cravats" and "London Cravat, Made in USA." $18–22

Two rayon ties with floral and leaf patterns, no labels. $18–25

Two ties made of rayon with leaf designs and geometric print labeled "by Haband." $18–22

Four-toned leaf print tie made of silk labeled "Gems of American Forestry, Woodland Prints, Cheney Cravats." Tri-colored abstract jungle print labeled "Van Heusen, Van Cruise." $20–25

Rayon jacquard tie with colorful leaf print, no label. $18–22

Large leaf prints are scattered all over this beige and burgundy rayon jacquard tie, no label. $18–22

Two grey rayon ties with geometric print and leaf and acorn pattern, labeled "Original by Damon." $18–22

Rayon jacquard tie with leaf print by "Haband." $18–22

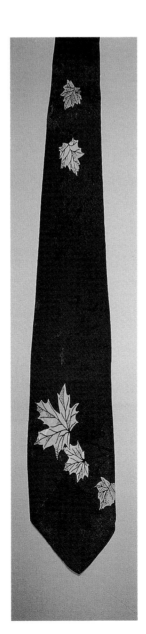

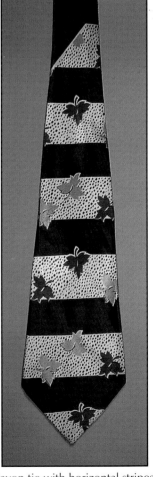

Designer tie made of silk with abstract leaf pattern signed "Schiaparelli." $35–50

Thin tie made of acetate with leaf print labeled "Beau Brummell." $15–20

Rayon tie with horizontal stripes and added leaf decoration, no label. $18–22

Exotics, Palm Trees, Flamingos

Cream-colored tie with hand painted palm tree and sail boat design. The back of the tie reads "Hand Painted by Rapson." $30–35

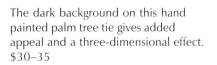

Oriental print ties from Manhattan Shirt Company, January 1947.

Blue rayon tie with deep-red palm tree; the back of the tie reads "An Original by Merlé." $25–35

The dark background on this hand painted palm tree tie gives added appeal and a three-dimensional effect. $30–35

Rayon tie with palm tree print labeled "Coast to Coast, National Shirt Shops, Miami Beach." $25–35

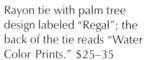

Rayon tie with palm tree design labeled "Regal"; the back of the tie reads "Water Color Prints." $25–35

Two hand painted palm tree ties, one with a sailboat and the other with flamingos, no labels. $30–40

Palm tree and ocean scene on a Photo tie; the back of the tie reads "Tropical Palm, Tru-Life Photie Prints." $35–50

Two exotic rayon ties with palm tree prints by "Haband" and "Wembley." $25–35

Orange and yellow palm tree tie labeled "Gold Crest, Styled by Robert Warurck, Hand Crafted." $25–35

Hand painted tie with flamingo and palm tree design labeled "Hand Screened Florida Creations." $25–35

Hand painted palm tree tie, no label. $30–35

Purple and pink palm tree tie labeled "Richards Cravats." $25–35

"Aloha Hawaii" tie and matching handkerchief with hand painted hula dancer, no label. $40–50 (set)

Three-toned satin tie with Southwestern print labeled "Wembley, King Louis Satin, A Rayon Fabric of Celanese Yarn." $20–25

"Bagdad Motifs" by Arrow, January 1947.

Four-toned rayon tie with flamingo print, no label. $30–35

Hand painted tie with sailboat design and polka dot embellishment, no label. $25–30

Rayon tie with sailboat design labeled "Helmsley King." $25–30

Hand painted tie made of rayon jacquard with golfing theme labeled "The Legath Cravat." $25–30

Outdoor, Deer, Fishing

Hand painted tie with scenic design labeled "Towncraft Cravats." $25–35

Navy blue tie with hand painted deer design labeled "Pennleigh." $25–35

Hand painted rayon tie with deer design, no label. $25–35

Burgundy rayon tie with deer and bird designs labeled "Fashion Craft Cravats." $25–30

Dark burgundy tie with hand painted deer design labeled "Pennleigh." $25–30

Rayon tie with hand painted fish design titled "What a Catch!", no label. $25–35

Hand painted rayon tie with leaping deer design. The lining of the tie is stamped "Resisto Tie, Sterling, Perfect Knotting, Wear Resisting Cravat, Supreme in Quality and Construction." $25–35

Rayon tie with deer print labeled "London Cravat." $20–30

Burgundy tie with a swordfish design in an allover pattern, no label. $22–28

Another version of "What a Catch!", the store label reads "Braude's, Atlantic City, N.J.". $25–35

Rayon jacquard tie with aquatic theme labeled "Sir by Botany." $25–35

Rayon tie with seahorse
motif by "Haband." $22–30

Green rayon tie with
allover donkey print
labeled "Marshall
Field & Company."
$25–30

Silk repp tie with hand
screened lily pad design,
no label. $25–30

Four-toned rayon tie with
zebra print labeled "Ward
& Ward." $25–35

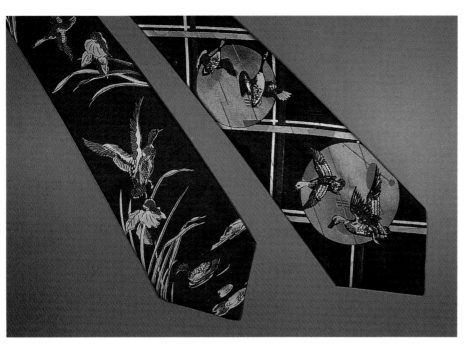

Silk tie with a bird pattern on a geometric background, no label; rayon tie titled "Mallard Duck" by "Arrow." $22–28

Four-toned rayon tie titled "The Great Outdoors" by "Ward & Ward." $25–30

Navy blue rayon tie with pheasant design, no label. $22–28

Two identical rayon ties in different color combinations titled "Humming Bird by Raxon" labeled "Morro Custom Cravats." $25–30

Rayon tie with parrot print labeled "Panel's King Size Resilient." $25–35

Rayon tie with peacock pattern marked "Individually hand painted." $30–35

This beautiful peacock design on grey rayon jacquard bears no label. $25–30

Navy rayon tie with allover bird design labeled "Pilgrim Cravats." $22–28

Yellow hand painted hunters' tie labeled "Diplomat." $28–35

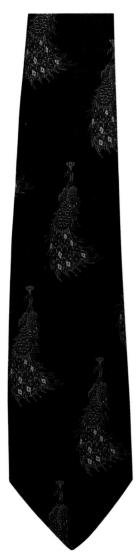

Navy blue polyester tie
with allover peacock
design labeled "Pace
Setter." This tie is from the
1970s. $15–20

Rayon tie with hunting theme
labeled "Adam." The back of
the tie reads "Painted by hand
- Hunter's Delight." $25–30

Tie made of wool with allover
dog pattern labeled "Wembley."
$22–30

Rayon tie with hunting
scene, no label. $22–28

Burgundy tie with a dog racing team labeled "Beau Brummell." $25–30

Rayon jacquard tie with hunting dog and bird design, no label; hand painted tie with hunting dog and bird design labeled "Pilgrim Cravats." The back of this tie reads "Brush Tones, Individually Hand Painted." $30–35

Silk screened hunter's tie made of rayon, no label. $28–35

Right:
Rust-colored satin tie with hand painted portrait of "Buttons" the dog labeled "Bond Style Manor." $30–40

Four-toned rayon tie with dog theme titled "The Great Outdoors" labeled "Premier by Diplomat." $28–35

Western Themes

Another tie from the series "The Great Outdoors" by "Diplomat" featuring a horse racing theme. $30–35

Rayon jacquard tie with silk screened horse print labeled "Fashion Row Cravat." $30–35

Two silk screened horses decorate this rayon tie. The store label reads "Pomerantz, Phila. Pa." $30–35

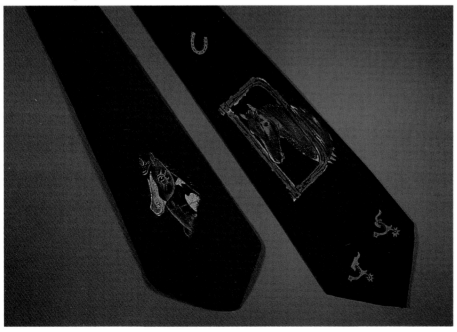

Two blue ties, one of rayon and one of wool, with hand painted horse head designs. The lighter blue tie is labeled "Sportie, hand painted in Colorful Colorado." $30–35

Western tie made of rayon with galloping horse motif, no label. $28–35

Five-toned rayon tie with horse head design within diagonal stripes labeled "Beau Brummell." $25–30

Pink and red rayon jacquard tie with rodeo rider design, no label. $28–35

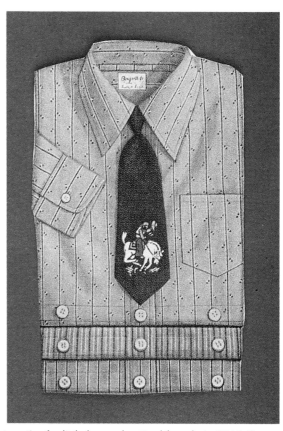

Western ties for little boys advertised for sale in 1946, Sears, Roebuck & Company.

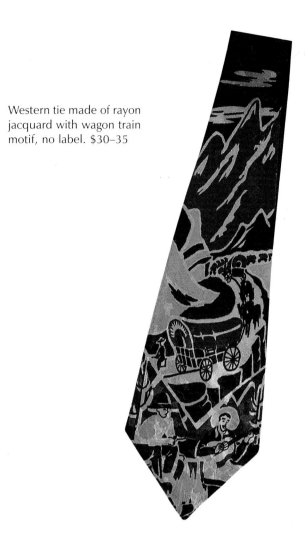

Western tie made of rayon jacquard with wagon train motif, no label. $30–35

"Frontier Prints" by Manhattan Ties, *Esquire*, December 1944.

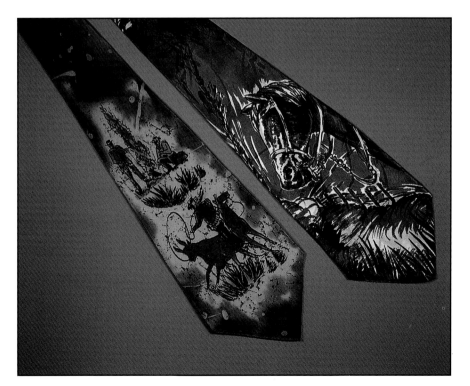

Hand painted silk tie with western theme, no label; rayon tie with horse design labeled "Kreway" and marked "Field & Stream Originals." $30–35

Two wagon train ties, one made of rayon and the other of acetate woven with nylon and marked "Hand painted in California." $30–35

Three hand painted western ties; the tie bands read "Monterey of California, Hand Painted in California." $30–35

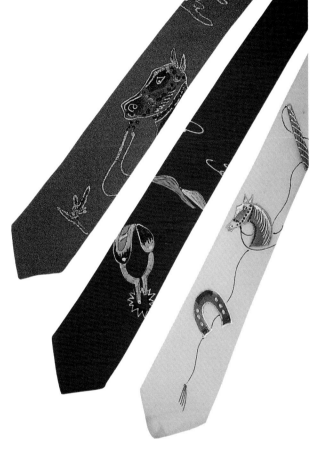

Two ties with desert and cactus motifs, one made of silk and the other made of rayon. $30–35

Bird design and western motif ties popular in 1948 as seen in Spiegel.

Western tie made of rayon labeled "Manhattan" with the original price tag of $2.50. $25–32

Rayon tie with small western designs, no label. $22–28

Rayon tie titled "Paul Revere" labeled "Arrow." $22–28

Thin tie made of rayon crepe with hand painted western theme, no label. $28–35

Novelties

Four-toned rayon tie with railroad and wagon train design labeled "Wilcrest American Pictorials, Wilson Bros." $22–28

Ad for the Miracle Tie by Superba made of 100% Dacron in 14 solid colors, *Esquire*, 1952.

Rayon tie titled "Timber - White Birch" labeled "Haband." $22–28

Novelty rayon tie decked out with playing cards, no label.

Rayon jacquard tie with top hat and champagne bottle print; the store label reads "Michael's, Hollywood, Calif." $25–35

Rust-colored rayon tie with Hawaiian print, no label. $22–28

A Middle Eastern theme is displayed on this blue rayon tie titled "Jewel of India" labeled "A Riviera Cravat, Designed in Paris." $22–28

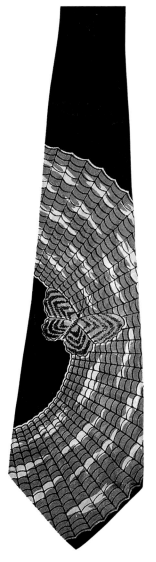

Rayon tie with Oriental motif, no label. $22–28

Four-toned rayon jacquard tie with butterfly design; the store label reads "Knickerbocker Haberdashers, New York." $22–28

Rayon tie with scenic print labeled "Eppo Ties from Fashion Center." $22–28

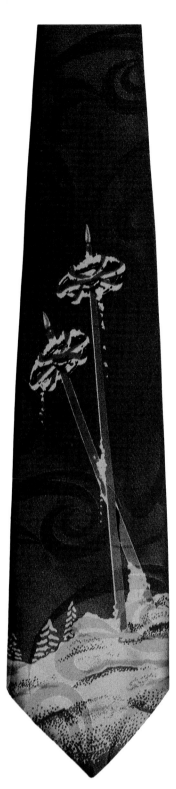

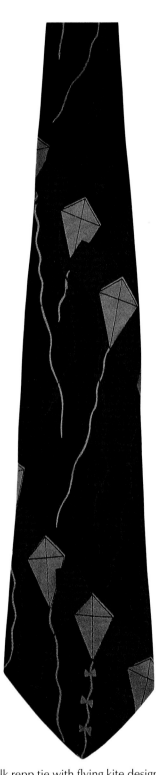

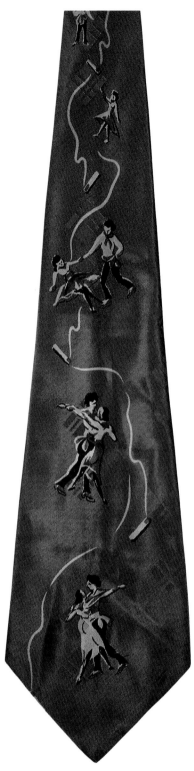

Burnt orange rayon jacquard tie titled "Winter Wonderland" and labeled "Haband." $25–30

Silk repp tie with flying kite designs; the store label reads "McAvoy, Boardwalk, Atlantic City." $25–30

Rayon jacquard tie with men and women doing different dance steps, no label. $28–35

Geometric designs decorate this green rayon tie; the store label reads "Gregory's, York, Pa." $25–30

Four-toned rayon tie with scenic print set into a diamond-pattern in the center of the tie. The label reads "Five Fold, A Better Cravat, Resilient Construction." $20–25

Hand painted promotional tie which reads "June is Dairy Month All Over America"; the tie is labeled "Scot Ties Ltd., Fifth Ave." $30–40

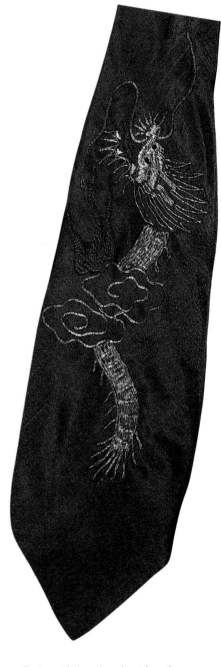

Three-toned rayon tie with abstract design labeled "Wembley, King Louis Satin, A Rayon Fabric of Celanese Yarn." $20–25

"Luck of the Irish" tie made of rayon, thin design, no label. $20–25

Japanese silk tie with hand embroidered dragon motif. $20–30

Hand Painted

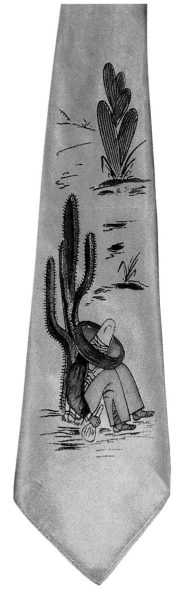

Hand painted purple satin tie depicting the front end of an early 1950s DeSoto. The back of the tie is signed by the artist Bill ???; the last name is partially worn off. $60–85

Hand painted tie depicting a Mexican in the desert, labeled "Arco, Luxury Ties, Selected Fabrics." $30–40

Rayon tie with hand painted portrait of the author's Mother, Marie Rodino, painted by a street artist in New York City in 1950. (Too rare to place a value)

Burgundy tie with hand painted winter scenes, no label;
Rayon tie with hand painted bird designs, no label. $30–40

Grey silk tie with hand painted
Oriental motif, no label. $35–45

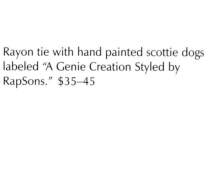

Rayon tie with hand painted scottie dogs
labeled "A Genie Creation Styled by
RapSons." $35–45

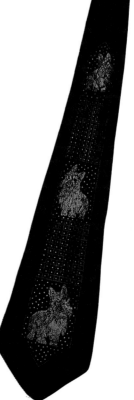

"Sweetheart" tie hand painted on rayon. The mirrored double image creates an unusual design. $30–40

Blue tie with hand painted leaf designs labeled "Acetate Rayon & Nylon, A Creation by Diane, Individually Hand Painted." $30–35

Two personalized neckties, one reads "David B. Prince" and the other reads "Jules J. Prince," both hand painted with mirrored images signed "dori." The paper tie bands read "Ty-Mode Cravats." $30–40

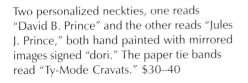

Hand painted tie with little boy and frog
and a brush stroke background labeled
"Jiffy Ties, Chicago." $35–45

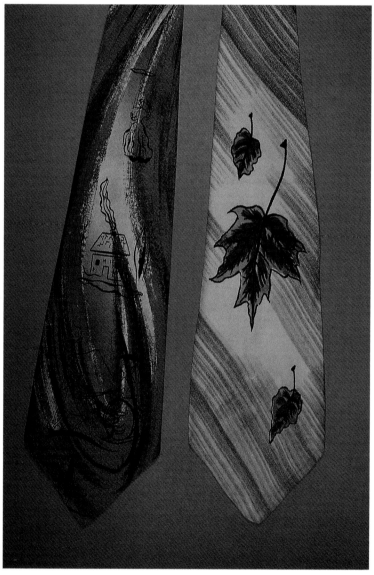

Two hand painted ties with brush stroke backgrounds, no labels.
$30–35

Hand painted initial tie labeled
"Arco Cravats." $28–35

Silk tie with air-brushed
abstract design labeled
"Superba Cravats."
$30–35

Two hand painted ties, one of silk and the other of rayon; the tie
with the climbing vines is labeled "Diplomat." $30–35

Rayon tie with abstract design
labeled "Hand Painted In
California." $30–35

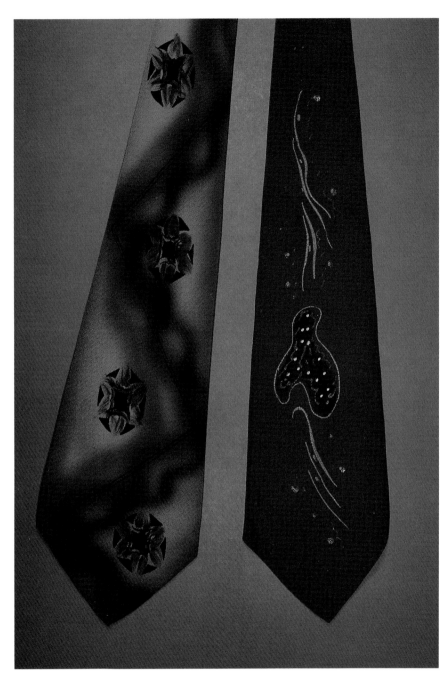

Two hand painted ties using air brush and brush stroke techniques; the air-brushed tie is labeled "Manhattan." $30–35

Hand painted silk tie with basket weave design labeled "Galét Originals, Beverly Hills, Calif." $30–35

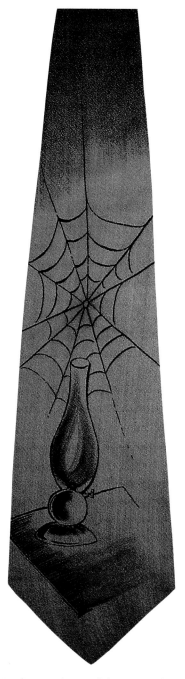

Hand painted tie with monkey in a palm tree, no label. $30–38

Hand painted tie with brush stroke design labeled "Beau Brummell." $28–35

Hand painted tie with lantern and spiderweb design, no label. $35–50

SKYLINE TIE was made from picture of New York's Chrysler building, visible beyond wearer's shoulder.

Photographic skyline tie; an innovative technique in the textile printing industry, as seen in *Life*, December 1947.

Ad for monogrammed silk ties by Leopold, circa 1953.

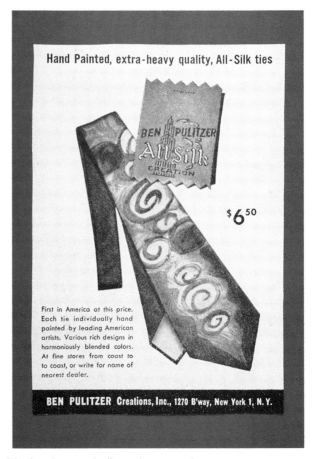

Hand painted ties personalized to order either with a picture of your automobile or your telephone number, circa 1953.

Ad for hand painted silk ties by Ben Pulitzer, January 1947.

Girlie and Peek-a-Boo

Rayon jacquard tie with mermaid print, no label. $35–50

Rayon jacquard tie with naked lady print, no label. $50–75

Rayon tie with bathing beauty print labeled "Titania, Hand Painted." $40–65

Lady Godiva tie made of rayon jacquard, no label. $40–60

Burgundy tie with hand painted design of a lady with a cigarette labeled "A Cutter Cravat Original." $35–50

Rayon jacquard tie with sitting nude design labeled "Fashion Row Cravat." $35–50

Wool tie with hand painted nude advertising Mercury Antennas, no label. $45–75

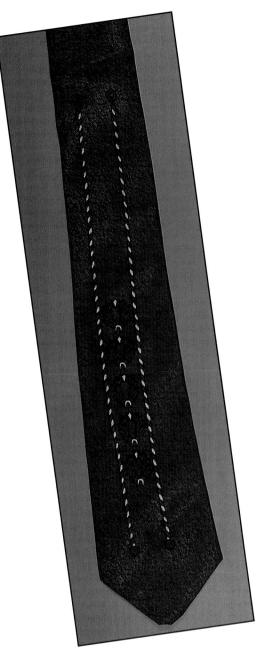

Front and back view of a peek-a-boo tie with a photo pin-up picture found on the lining of the necktie. The tie is marked "Glo-Vure Process, Belleville, N.J." $75–125

Cartoon illustration used for advertising Arrow shirts and ties for Father's Day, June 1949.

Hand painted peek-a-boo tie titled "Stars Above You" with a pin-up photo of a bathing beauty on the lining labeled "Hollyvogue Resilient, Made in California." $75–125

Green polyester tie labeled "Corsair, for brown and tan suits" featuring a pin-up girl on the lining. $60–100

Three different views of a normal looking checked tie with a photo of Jane Mansfield on the lining. $75–125

Two conservative striped ties, one of cotton and silk and the other of acetate, both revealing photos in the lining. $75–125

Designers

Hand painted silk necktie titled "The Modest Swans" signed "Dali" and labeled "Fashion Row." $300–500

Burgundy tie with abstract design signed "Dali" and labeled "Fashion Row Cravat, Sterling Quality." $300–500

Necktie signed "Dali" titled "Stage Backdrop" and labeled "Artcraft Creations; Another signed tie by "Dali" and labeled "Diplomat." This design was titled "Persian Butterflies." $300–500

"Proud Peacock" signed "Dali" and labeled "TowncraftDeLuxe"; "Paradise Wall" signed "Dali" and labeled "Fashion Craft Cravats"; "The Swan's Palace" signed "Dali" and labeled "Smoothie Imperial." $300–500

Three-toned silk tie with abstract print, signed and labeled "Countess Mara, New York." $40–65

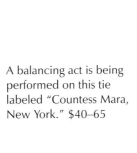

A balancing act is being performed on this tie labeled "Countess Mara, New York." $40–65

Squirrels and bees are found on these busy ties labeled "Countess Mara." Her initials are found on the front of the ties and sometimes incorporated into the design itself. $40–65

Three more silk ties signed and labeled "Countess Mara."
$40–65

Two identical ties in different color
combinations, similar to the artistic
designs of Countess Mara. These
neckties are titled "Horn Of Plenty"
and labeled "French Original, Pure
Silk." $40–60

Photo Ties

Cartoon illustration of a woman at the department store tie counter, *Apparel Arts*, May 1955.

Color photo tie titled "Happy Hunting" and labeled "Tru Val." $35–50

Photo tie titled "Tropical Palm" and labeled "Tru-Life Photie Prints." $40–65

Color photo necktie titled "Anglers Dream"
labeled "Sir by Botany." $35–50

Another "Color Photo" necktie titled "On the
Hook," no label. $35–50

Color photo necktie titled "The Water Fall" labeled "Tru-Life Photie Prints." $35–55

Another Color Photo tie titled "The Anglers Dream," no label. $35–50

A scenic view is featured on this 1970s version of a photo tie made of polyester labeled "Joe Namath for Arrow." $35–50

Color photo tie titled "Cathedral Window," no label. $35–50

Bibliography

Books

Chenoune, Farid. *A History of Men's Fashion*. Paris: Flammarion, 1993.

Colle, Doriece. *Collars...Stocks...Cravats*. Emmaus, Pennsylvania: Rodale Press Inc.

Dyer, Rod, and Ron Spark. *Fit To Be Tied: Vintage Ties of the Forties and Fifties*. New York: Abbeville Press, 1987.

Gibbings, Sarah. *The Tie: Trends and Traditions*. New York: Studio Editions, Ltd., 1990.

Montana, Hunter, and Shelkie Montana. *Cowboy Ties*. Salt Lake City: Gibbs-Smith Publisher, 1994.

Mosconi, Davide, and Riccardo Villarosa. *The Book of Ties*. London, England: Tie Rack Ltd., 1985.

Wilson, William, and the Editors of *Esquire* magazine. *Man At His Best: The Esquire Guide To Style*. Addison-Wesley Publishing Company, 1985.

Catalogs

Adolph Levy & Son, Spring-Summer 1902.

Aldens, 1967. Ben Silver Collection, Spring, 1995.

Brooks Brothers, Autumn, 1995.

Baird-North Company, 1918-1919.

Butler Brothers, 1937.

Charles William Stores, Inc., 1925.

Chicago Mail Order Company, 1911-1912, 1934, 1935.

Klausner & Co., 1896, 1898.

Men's Wear, August 10, 1898, March 8, 1899.

Montgomery Ward, 1922, 1937, 1938.

National Bellas Hess, 1928. National Cloak and Suit Company, 1925.

Sears, Roebuck and Company, 1900, 1908, 1909, 1930, 1937, 1942, 1943-1944, 1946-1947, 1949.

Spiegel, 1948.

Periodicals

Apparel Arts, May, June, July, August, September, October, December, 1955; May, June, July, November, 1956; January, February, March, April, 1957.

Esquire, September, 1934; October, December, 1935; January, July, 1937; July, October, November, 1938; April, May, June, October, 1939; May, 1940; November, 1942; March, 1943; December, 1944; April, 1945; January, 1947; October, 1951; August, 1952; December, 1953; October, 1954.

Gentleman's Quarterly, Summer, Fall, Winter, 1957; Spring, Summer, 1958.

Life, September, October, 1940; March, December, 1947; November, 1949; December, 1963; March, 1967; December, 1978.

Saturday Evening Post, June 30, 1928; September 22, November 17, 1928; June 1, 1929; April 12, 1930; August 23, 1930; September 20, 1930; May 30, 1942; November 4, 1950.